URBAN BIKERS'
TRICKS & TIPS

LOW-TECH & NO-TECH ways to FIND, RIDE, & KEEP a BICYCLE

by Dave Glowacz (Mr.Bike)
www.mrbike.com

GRAPHIC DESIGN BY
Gladys Rosa-Mendoza (Rosa+Wesley Design, Wheaton IL)

ILLUSTRATED BY
Bacon Friar, Dave Glowacz, Phil Gullett, Tara Hoffmann
Eric Masi, Kristin Mount, Josh Neufeld,
Chuck Quint (represented by Artisan Chicago),
Soo Spencer, Mike Werner, Aaron White

PHOTOGRAPHY BY
Bacon Friar, Dave Glowacz

ELECTRONIC IMAGING BY
Jeff Grunewald, Alex Wilson

DESIGN PRODUCTION BY
Maria Jose Barandarian, Christopher Yu

MANAGING EDITOR
J.Raymond Nanczek

ASSOCIATE EDITOR
Nadia Oehlsen

ASSISTANT EDITOR
Lisa Phillips

Wordspace Press
CHICAGO
www.wordspacepress.com

URBAN BIKERS' TRICKS & TIPS

low-tech & no-tech ways to FIND, RIDE, & KEEP a BICYCLE

Dave Glowacz (Mr. Bike)

Warning and Disclaimer

The purpose of this book is to educate and entertain. However, as with any physical activity, bicycling can lead to injury or death. Therefore, every person should learn and practice accepted bike-safety methods before trying any of the tips contained in this book. Persons using information from this book also assume all rights and responsibilities for their own actions. The author and Wordspace Press have neither liability nor responsibility to any person or entity with respect to any loss or damage caused, or alleged to have been caused, directly or indirectly, by the information contained in this book. The reader understands and agrees to absolve the author, the publisher, and their agents, be they individuals or organizations, singly or collectively, of all blame for any injury, misadventure, harm, loss, or inconvenience suffered as a result of using the information in this book. If you do not wish to be bound by the above, you may return this book to the publisher for a full refund.

Publisher's Cataloging in Publication
(Provided by Quality Books, Inc.)

Glowacz, Dave.
    Urban bikers' tricks & tips : low-tech & no-tech ways to find, ride, & keep a bicycle /
by Dave Glowacz (Mr. Bike) ; illustrated by Bacon Friar ... [et al.] ; photography by Bacon Friar,
Dave Glowacz. -- 3rd rev. ed.
    p. cm.
    Urban bikers' tricks and tips
    Includes index.
    ISBN-13: 9780965172820
    ISBN-10: 0965172821
    ISBN-13: 9780965172837
    ISBN-10: 096517283X
    [etc.]
    1. Cycling. 2. Cycling--Safety measures. 3. Bicycles--Purchasing. I. Title. II. Title: Urban bikers' tricks
and tips.

GV1043.7.G56 2010   796.6
                QBI10-600100

Table of Contents

TABLE OF CONTENTS

A Message from Mr. Bike

Think of the bicycling you did as a kid. Liberating and fun, right?

Now think about bicycling in the hard, fast metro area where you live: the potholes, the car-clogged lanes, the mad green-light scramble, the car doors that open in your face. Sure, you'd bring your bike into all of that—on the carrying rack anchored to the back of your car.

What about people who actually ride their bikes in heavy traffic? Maybe you've seen one: She glides past you and all the vehicles around you. She's not racing, but she gets around a double-parked car here, a pothole there. She either knows something you don't, or she's nuts.

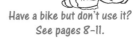

Have a bike but don't use it?
See pages 8–11.

And you've heard how often bikes get ripped off. When you see bikes locked up all over town, you figure they keep the cops and lock makers pretty busy.

Or, one cold or rainy day, you spot a cyclist in traffic. He's not wearing one of those fancy jackets or Gore-Tex pants—yet he looks pretty comfortable.

Could you learn to do any of that stuff?

Maybe—if you pored over all the slick bike magazines you've seen. But you don't *want* to sit and read. Nor do you want to buy cycling clothes, parts, tools . . . it'd be nice just to ride your bike as easily as when you were a kid.

That's where my book comes in.

How do people manage to bike to the office? See pages 228–231.

My book gives you the secrets behind everything we've just described, and more—without making you spend lots of time or money.

My book tells you only what you need to know to bike confidently and efficiently in the streets of your town. Much of it came from experienced cyclists, police officers, and manufacturers—and isn't written anywhere else.

Most of what you might need is here.

Got a fear of traffic?
See pages 64–65.

(continued on next page)

I

Like, what type of bike (of the many kinds out there) is best for you? Or what do you do about the little things that go wrong, like flat tires? And how do you protect yourself from thieves, motorists, and bad weather?

Or, if you already ride a lot, what are some cool tricks that the urban gear-heads know—like how to time lights or jump over stuff?

My book tells you exactly what to do in every case.

Hard for you to choose a bike or parts?
See pages 4 and 14.

Did I say "tells?" I meant "shows": This book uses pictures more than almost any other book on cycling. Flip open to any page and you'll see.

And because you and I want to have fun, I got some hip folks to do the drawings—guys and gals who have more fun with a pencil than most people have with their entire bodies.

But this isn't a coloring book. I leave the kid's stuff for grade-school bike rodeos. Like when I diagram the four ways to make an urban right turn: At least two are trickier than something a child should ever do.

Don't get the wrong idea. I don't tell you how to charge head-on into traffic, zoom onto the sidewalk, then lock your bike with a 30-pound chain. The secrets I give you involve a little trick here and there, plus a lot of what some call stealth.

Most of these tips are interesting enough on their own. But you wouldn't sit still too long if someone just recited them to you. "Uh-uh," you'd say, crossing your arms and jutting your chin. "*Show* me your bike tricks."

Well . . . turn the page.

Want to make your bike fly?
See pages 164-165.

CHOOSING A BIKE

Buying a bike can be tough. It seems like there are **too many styles**. But unless you're a racer, you don't care about small differences. And **most bikes have only a few big differences between them**. This chapter shows you.

Page 10

So which style of bike's right for you? You only have to **ask yourself how and where you ride**. This chapter asks you—then, based on the answers, tells you the kind of bike you need.

Page 5

What if you already have a bike? Perhaps it seems too old, or it doesn't feel right. Should you get a new one? Maybe not.

Page 11

Take a look at this chapter to learn whether you should fix up your old bike, and how to do it. But **if you do decide to get a new bike**, this chapter tells you what to watch out for.

Page 12

What about all that extra stuff: bike bags, water bottles, pumps? What do you really need? This chapter tells you that, too.

Speaking of extra stuff, **why would you want dozens of gears** on your bike? What are you missing without all those gears? Mystery solved here.

Page 17

Page 20

16 X 1⅜

Also, you've probably seen your kind of bike with wider, narrower, or knobbier tires. **Would you like to try different tires?** Read this chapter first.

Page 22

CHOOSING A

The four basic bike types

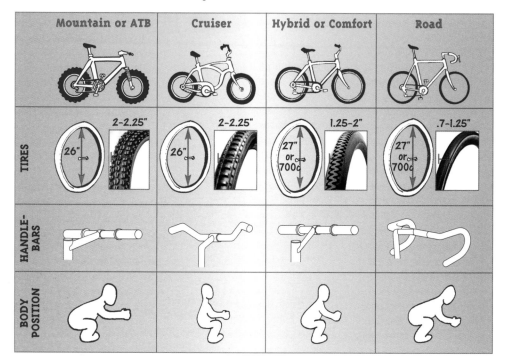

	Mountain or ATB	Cruiser	Hybrid or Comfort	Road
TIRES	26" — 2–2.25"	26" — 2–2.25"	27" or 700c — 1.25–2"	27" or 700c — .7–1.25"
HANDLE-BARS				
BODY POSITION				

Other kinds of bikes

WOMEN'S BIKES

Shorter frame height
Why: **Women** (on average) are shorter than men

Shorter handlebar height

Handlebars not as far forward

Shorter frame length

Why: Women have shorter torsos and more arm stress

Have your bike dealer order from suppliers listed under "Bicycles, women's" in Appendix B.

FOLDING BIKES

WHY & WHY NOT

👍 Easily taken on buses, trains, planes

👍 Easily stored in small spaces

👍 Good for travelling and multi-modal commutes

Have your bike dealer order from suppliers listed under "Bicycles, folding" in Appendix B.

BIKE TYPE

Which bike is made for you?

STOP HERE AND READ

In most bike stores you'll find four kinds of bikes. How are they different? Mostly in tire size, handlebar height and style, and the sitting position they put you in. Choosing the one that's right for you depends on how and where you ride.

How you ride	Bike type you should ride WHY: T=tire, P=position, G=single-speed gear			
	Mtn	Cruiser	Hybrid	Road
over curbs	T	T		
in an upright position		P	P	
don't watch the road	T	T	T	
on roads with glass and potholes	T	T	T	
long distances			T	T, P
lots of short runs	T	T		
mainly on concrete		T	T	T
mainly on dirt	T		T	
on both dirt and concrete	T		T	
on hills	T, P		T, P	T, P
don't use gears		G		G
on wet pavement	T	T	T	
fast			T, P	T, P
in lots of wind				T, P

Light bikes

Don't worry about the weight of your bike unless:
➤ You often must carry it up stairs
➤ You ride up lots of steep hills
➤ You race

If you must have a light bike, remember that cruisers weigh the most. As for other bike types, you can get lighter models simply by paying more.

In addition to multi-gear, you can get single-gear road bikes (also called track bikes and fixies).

RECUMBENTS

WHY & WHY NOT

👍 Leaning back is less stressful on upper body

👍 Reclining position gives your legs more power

👎 Most recumbent riders can't see over tops of cars

👎 On older models, front wheel wobbles more when you start

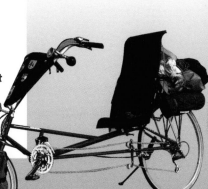

On recumbent bikes, you sit back as you would on a lawn chair. This posture takes the stress off of your back, arms, and neck.

SPENDING

Buy new, used, or keep old?

Situation	Do this
You don't own a usable bike and: ➢ You haven't ridden a bike for a while. ➢ You won't ride often. ➢ You want to spend less than $100.	 Buy a used bike.
➢ Fixing your current bike costs more than $100 (see page 7). ➢ Keeping an old bike working costs too much because you're using it more than you'd expected. ➢ You have plenty of money but no bike.	 Buy a new bike.
You can make your current bike fit you and it does what you want.	 Keep your current bike.
You often ride through bad weather (and especially salt) and you don't mind recycling.	 Get a used bike every year and recycle the old one.

STOP HERE AND READ

How much should you spend on a bike? You can spend $50-100 for a used bike that'll last a long time if you take good care of it. On the other hand, you can buy a decent new bike for several hundred dollars.

The more you ride, the more you should spend—but not for the bike itself! Instead:

➤ Buy accessories (like a carrying rack) that help you use your bike more often. (See page 14.)

➤ Invest in good locks, because you can then leave your bike unattended more often. (See page 52.)

➤ Invest in maintenance when the bike breaks or parts wear down.

➤ If you haven't ridden in a while, start out with a cheap used bike to see how much you'll use it.

Danger

If you spend too little:

➤ Once you learn how easy it is to get around, you might end up using that bike more than you'd thought.

➤ You buy junk, then find yourself not riding because the bike's broken or hard to ride.

➤ You end up without accessories that would make you more comfortable with riding: helmet, lock, lights.

Smart Ideas

➤ You can find a decent used bike for $50. After a few years, when you've trashed it, give it to your favorite bike recycler.

➤ Look for classified ads from rich but foolish young professionals who dump their expensive bikes, cheap, when they move.

➤ Scout garage sales and auctions.

➤ Some bike shops train kids to fix bikes. And some towns offer free bikes to the public. Contact your local advocacy group (see Appendix A) to find out. If your town has such programs, donate your old bike.

➤ Some credit unions offer low-interest or no-interest loans for buying bikes. Search on-line for "bicycle loans" and "credit union."

MAKING YOUR

Typical fit problems

STOP HERE AND READ

Lots of people have bikes that don't fit right. Usually the frame is too tall, short, or long. A bad fit can hurt your back, neck, or shoulders. Or it can just make you feel strange. So should you get a different bike? Maybe not. First decide whether moving the handlebars and/or seat will fix the problem.

Bending head up hurts neck

Leaning over hurts back

Too much stretching hurts shoulders

Too much weight hurts arms

Too much knee bend hurts legs
(Knee pain can also result from not shifting gears. See p. 20.)

CURRENT BIKE
FIT YOU

TILTING THE SEAT

Why: Put more or less weight on your crotch or arms

To take some weight off the front of your crotch and put more on your arms, tilt the seat slightly nose-down.

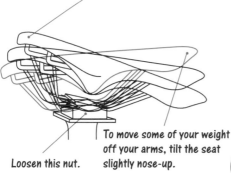

Loosen this nut.

To move some of your weight off your arms, tilt the seat slightly nose-up.

MOVING THE SEAT FORWARD

Why: Puts you closer to the handlebars for less stretch

1 Loosen the seat nut.

2 Push the seat forward.

3 Tighten the nut.

*Sore butt? **See page 11.***

RAISING THE SEAT

Why: With the correct knee bend you pedal easier

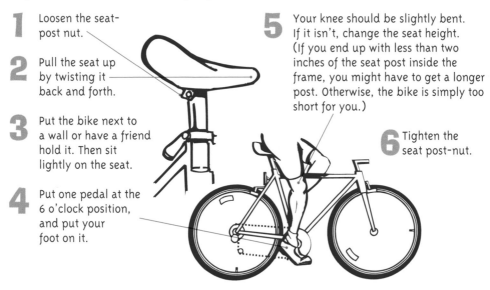

1 Loosen the seat-post nut.

2 Pull the seat up by twisting it back and forth.

3 Put the bike next to a wall or have a friend hold it. Then sit lightly on the seat.

4 Put one pedal at the 6 o'clock position, and put your foot on it.

5 Your knee should be slightly bent. If it isn't, change the seat height. (If you end up with less than two inches of the seat post inside the frame, you might have to get a longer post. Otherwise, the bike is simply too short for you.)

6 Tighten the seat post-nut.

Adjusting the handlebars

Trick #1 is easiest. If it doesn't work try #2, then #3. But for #2 and #3 you have to take apart you handlebar assembly. If you don't know how, ask a bike mechanic to do it for you.

STOP HERE AND READ

WHY

👍 You sit straighter and don't stretch as far

1 Raising your current stem
Loosen the bolt at the top of your handlebar stem. By twisting the handlebars, pull them up to a comfortable position. If they won't get there without leaving two inches of stem inside the frame, you should replace or extend your handlebar stem.

2"

2 Extending your stem
Get a handlebar stem riser. Risers come in several heights and diameters. Installing one requires a socket wrench with a six-inch extension, and you might have to replace some cables. (Have your bike dealer order the Pyramid Stem Riser from J&B distributors, listed under "Handlebar parts" in Appendix B.)

3 Replacing your stem
Get a stem that goes higher or closer to your body.

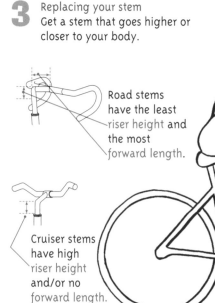

Road stems have the least riser height and the most forward length.

Cruiser stems have high riser height and/or no forward length.

ATB stems (for mountain and cross/hybrid bikes) have moderate riser length and height.

Fixing a sore butt

If you haven't bicycled in a while, expect to get a sore butt or crotch or chafed thighs. After you've ridden regularly, chafing or soreness should go away.

 Danger
The widest and softest seats give your butt the most comfort. But if the seat's too wide, it'll rub the inside of your thighs. And if it's too soft your hips might rock—making your thighs chafe.

IF SORENESS DOESN'T STOP

1 Check the seat height and tilt (see page 9).

2 Try a different seat.

gel-filled

middle groove or slit

slim tip and raised back

spring-cushioned

wide rear

split

3 Use padded or seamless cycling shorts with no underwear.

4 Wear low-friction cycling briefs. (Seams in regular underwear cause friction.)

5 If friction persists (especially for women):
➢ Apply baby powder to both your body and shorts before cycling.
➢ Apply a skin toughener, such as Preparation H, to the areas that make seat contact. Apply before you go to bed, not before you ride.

6 For rashes, infections, or excessive discharges:
➢ Use shorts with a cotton strip, to absorb moisture.
➢ Before riding, use a moisture barrier such as Desitin.

Buying a NEW BIKE

After you've decided what kind of new bike you want (see pages 4 and 5), it's time to go to the bike store. But there are a few things you should know to help you make the purchase.

Before you shop

KNOW YOUR LIMIT

Decide on your spending limit for each of these

🚲	The bicycle itself
	Accessories such as carrying racks and patch kits (see page 14)
	Locks (see page 52)

WEAR YOUR BIKE CLOTHES

Do you plan to wear the same kind of clothes whenever you ride? If so, you might want to wear them when you look for a new bike. It'll help you get the right fit.

Smart Idea
Many bike stores cut prices in the fall. This is the best time of year for a good deal on a new bike.

At the bike store

BODY POSITION

Take the bike for a test ride and check these items.

Smart Idea
If a bike salesperson won't spend time to help you get the right fit, buy your bike elsewhere. See page 34 for tips on choosing a bike shop.

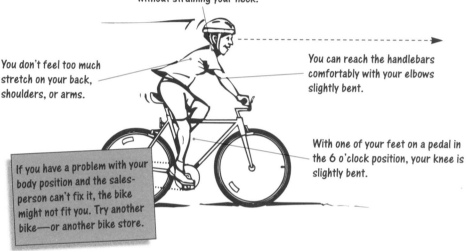

You can look straight ahead easily without straining your neck.

You don't feel too much stretch on your back, shoulders, or arms.

You can reach the handlebars comfortably with your elbows slightly bent.

With one of your feet on a pedal in the 6 o'clock position, your knee is slightly bent.

If you have a problem with your body position and the salesperson can't fix it, the bike might not fit you. Try another bike—or another bike store.

SORE BUTT

When you buy your bike, ask the salesperson if you can exchange the seat later—in case you find it uncomfortable. But, after you've ridden for a few weeks, what if your butt doesn't stop hurting? See page 11.

On a woman's frame (or any frame without a horizontal top tube), ask the salesperson to fit you.

FRAME HEIGHT

The first thing you should check on a bike is the frame height. On a bike made for men, stand with the bike between your legs, just in front of the seat. Measure the space between the top tube and your crotch. For urban riding, you want a one- to three-inch space.

WHAT ACCESSORIES DO YOU NEED?

Item	Needed if you:	For more info see page
aluminum wheels	ride in rain, so need quick stops on wet rims	219
ankle strap	wear long pants, no chain guard	233
armrests	ride far in bent-over posture	15
axle pegs	transport another adult short distances	17
basket	carry stuff occasionally	17
bungee cords	carry stuff occasionally	16
carrying rack	carry stuff occasionally	16
chain cover	ride often in rain or snow	219
fenders	protect clothes if ride often in rain or snow	222
foam grips	have hand numbness or wrist pain	15
glasses or goggles	ride in dusty or insect-filled air, or wear contacts	233
gloves	have hand numbness	15
handlebar bag	use maps often, carry stuff occasionally	17
handlebar ends	sometimes need less wind resistance	15
helmet	fall, so you won't smash your head	226
kerchief	wipe hands after bike adjustment, face after hot ride	233
key holder or chain	ride without pockets or bags	233
kickstand	park your bike, or add or remove baggage	189
lights	ride at night	212
locks	want security	52
mirrors	feel uncomfortable about what's behind	68
noise makers	need to be obvious	76
panniers	carry stuff often	17
pump	bike far from gas stations	30
quick-release seat	hit on ceilings, or fear theft	18
quick-release wheels	remove wheels often	18
reflectors	ride at night	210
seat bag	carry tools only	17
tire liners	get tire punctures	31
toe clips	ride hills, or go very fast or far	19
trailers	carry big stuff often	16
water bottle	bike long distances or in hot weather	19

STOP HERE AND READ

When you spend money on a bike, you should budget something for accessories. Why? Some of these extras can make your biking a lot easier. This list shows you what you might need and why.

HANDLEBAR
ACCESSORIES

ACCESSORY MOUNT

WHY & WHY NOT

👍 If you have lots of gadgets (brake levers, gear shift levers, light, computer, bell), they'll crowd your handlebars.

👎 A thief can steal everything on the accessory bar just by taking the bar.

Shown: Multi-purpose accessories mount. Order direct from TerraCycle (listed under "Handlebar parts" in Appendix B).

ARMRESTS

WHY & WHY NOT

👍 When you ride long distances, they let you lean your forearms onto the handlebars.

👍 They make wind hit you less, and they take weight off of your wrists and hands.

👍 They are easily clipped on and off.

HANDLEBAR ENDS

WHY & WHY NOT

👍 On straight handlebars, bar ends let you lean forward so wind hits you less. And they make it easier to change your hand position.

FOAM GRIPS OR BIKE GLOVES

WHY & WHY NOT

👍 They cushion your hands to stop pain and numbness.

👎 Cheap ones wear through easily.

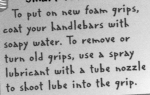

Smart Idea
To put on new foam grips, coat your handlebars with soapy water. To remove or turn old grips, use a spray lubricant with a tube nozzle to shoot lube into the grip.

BAGGAGE

Carrying racks and bungee cords

WHY & WHY NOT

👍 A carrying rack lets you carry stuff much more conveniently than you could in your arms or in a backpack.

With enough bungee cords, you can strap on really big loads.

net strap

Carrying racks attach to your bike in two places:

behind the seat post

next to the rear axle

adjustable bungee

multi-strap

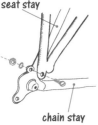

INSTALLATION

What if your bike doesn't have the right holes for mounting a carrying rack? Don't worry. You can get hardware that adapts your bike frame to hold the rack. Order clips, brackets, and extenders from a distributor listed under "Hardware" in Appendix B.

Make sure the rack doesn't get in the way of the brake cable

seat stay

chain stay

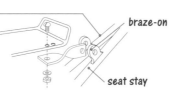

braze-on

seat stay

Attaching a rack to a bike with existing holes

seat stay

seat-stay bridge

seat stay

chain stay

Attaching a rack to a bike using extra hardware

seat post

Trailers

WHY & WHY NOT

👍 Can carry really big stuff.

👎 Needs installation, trickier to ride.

ACCESSORIES

Other carrying items

BASKETS

Smart Idea
To keep stuff from rattling around, put in a large, flat sponge.

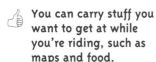

AXLE PEGS

Axle pegs (also known as free-style pegs) come in different sizes. Before you buy pegs, ask your bike dealer to check your axle size.

WHY & WHY NOT

 Lets you carry another person for short distances.

 You can't install one on a quick-release wheel.

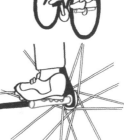

HANDLEBAR BAGS

WHY & WHY NOT

 You can carry stuff you want to get at while you're riding, such as maps and food.

SEAT BAGS

WHY & WHY NOT

You want to carry only tools or other small stuff in a bag that's easy to take with you when you leave your bike unattended.

PANNIERS

WHY & WHY NOT

Make it easy to carry lots of stuff often.

Not cheap. If you carry stuff less often, get side baskets.

Easily clip on and off your bike

Usually come in pairs: use two for long trips, one for daily commuting

How to modify:

➤ add shoulder strap
➤ waterproof them with a spray

Carries lots of stuff

Side pockets for stuff you pull out often

QUICK-RELEASE
ACCESSORIES

Quick-release seat

WHY & WHY NOT

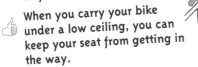

👍 When you leave your bike, you can easily remove the seat to avoid theft.

👍 When you carry your bike under a low ceiling, you can keep your seat from getting in the way.

👎 When you leave your bike, you always have to take the seat with you or use a seat lock.

Quick-release wheels

WHY & WHY NOT

👍 If you often remove your wheel for fixing or locking, you can remove it more easily.

💡 **Smart Idea**
Don't avoid quick-release wheels because you think they're easier to steal. A thief with a wrench can just as easily remove nut-fastened wheels. Always lock through both your wheels!

HOW TO ATTACH A QUICK-RELEASE WHEEL

1 Flip the quick-release lever so that its inner side faces out.

2 Stand the bike upside down. Place the wheel into the frame so that the quick-release lever is on your left as you stand in front of the bike.

3 On the back wheel of a bike with a rear derailleur: to get the axle past the chain, you might have to pull the derailleur back.

4 Work the axle into the frame by pushing down on both sides. If the axle won't go in, unscrew the axle nut slightly: With one hand, hold the quick-release lever. With the other hand, grab the nut on the other side of the wheel. Unscrew the nut a quarter turn (counter-clockwise as you face it).

POWER ACCESSORIES

Toe clips & clipless pedals

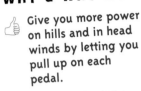

WHY & WHY NOT

👍 Give you more power on hills and in head winds by letting you pull up on each pedal.

👎 Toe clips don't let you wear all kinds of shoes.

👎 Toe clips don't let you take your foot off the pedal as easily as when you don't have them.

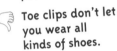

Water bottle

WHY & WHY NOT

👍 You ride long distances or in hot weather, when it's important that you drink water.

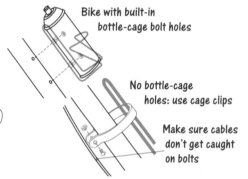

Bike with built-in bottle-cage bolt holes

No bottle-cage holes: use cage clips

Make sure cables don't get caught on bolts

---

5 After you've gotten the axle all the way in, turn the quick-release lever to a three o'clock position.

6 With one hand, apply the brakes to the wheel and hold them tightly. With the other hand, close the quick-release lever: flip it so that its outer side faces out. Then release the brake.

7 The lever is closed when it gets parallel to the chain stay, and it should close tightly. If the lever doesn't close all the way, flip the lever back open. Unscrew the axle nut (counterclockwise as you face it) a quarter turn. Then try to close the lever again. If you can easily close the lever past the point where it's parallel to the chain stay, flip the lever back open. Screw the axle nut in (clockwise as you face it) lightly, until you feel it resist your effort. Then try to close the lever again.

YES

NO NO

8 Give the wheel a slow spin. (Spin the back wheel forward so the pedals don't move.) If the tire rubs against either chain stay or brake pad, open the quick-release lever. Move the wheel so the tire doesn't rub; hold it there, and close the lever. If you can't position the wheel in a way that keeps it from rubbing on a brake pad, you might have to open your brake slightly. (If you don't know how, get expert advice.)

chain stay

GEARS

Why have gears?

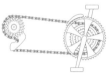  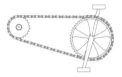

Multi-speed bike with
multiple front and back gears

Single-speed bike with
single front and back gears

WHY YOU SHOULD HAVE MULTIPLE GEARS

➢ You have a hard time getting started from a stop.
➢ On flat land, you want to accelerate quickly.
➢ You want to ride like a speed demon from Hell.
➢ You start and stop a lot or climb hills, and not having multiple speeds causes knee problems.
➢ You want easier pedaling on hills or in wind.

ARE MORE SPEEDS BETTER?

Not always. When a bike has more than 10 speeds, many of the speeds overlap each other. So while the bike you want might come with 21 speeds, you probably don't need (and won't use) them.

WHY YOU DON'T WANT MULTIPLE GEARS

➢ Multi-speed gear hardware—the derailleurs and cables—gets screwed up easily.

➢ Multi-speed gear hardware requires more maintenance—especially if you often park your bike outside or ride in snow.
➢ If you've always ridden single-speed bikes, it might be too much hassle to learn shifting.
➢ If you haven't used multi-speed gears and don't have a problem pedaling, you don't need them.

ALTERNATIVES TO MULTI-SPEED BIKES

➢ Buy a single-speed bike.
➢ Turn your multi-speed bike into a single-speed bike. Have a mechanic remove the derailleurs and shorten the chain.
➢ Buy a bike with a multi-speed internal-gear hub. They need adjustment less often.

Gearing for hills: a granny gear

If you ride often on tough hills, get a bike whose front gears include a granny gear. When you shift to the granny gear, you pedal faster but with less force than you do with your other gears.

STANDARD FRONT GEARS

Smallest gear has 24 to 28 teeth

Mid-sized gear has 32 to 40 teeth

Largest gear has 42 to 53 teeth

Double chainring

Triple chainring

FRONT GEARS WITH GRANNY GEAR

Smallest gear has 20 or 22 teeth

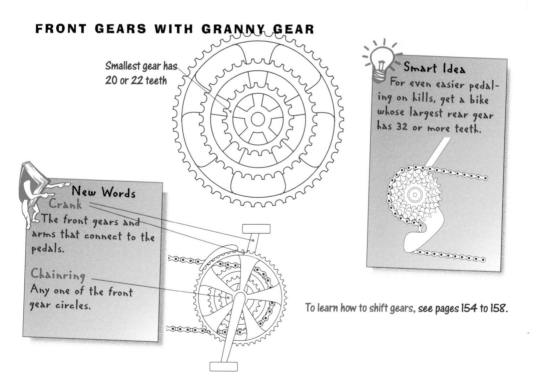

Smart Idea
For even easier pedaling on hills, get a bike whose largest rear gear has 32 or more teeth.

New Words
Crank
The front gears and arms that connect to the pedals.

Chainring
Any one of the front gear circles.

To learn how to shift gears, see pages 154 to 158.

TIRES

Tire size

STOP HERE AND READ

Some people replace the tires that came on their bike with skinnier or wider tires —usually because they want a tougher tire or they want to pedal more easily. If you want to replace your tires with a different kind, check here to find out which to get—and what to watch out for.

HOW TIRES ARE MEASURED

Tire size usually appears on the side

➤ First number: diameter
➤ Second number: width
➤ Numbers may be shown in millimeters (two or three digits) or inches (one or two digits)

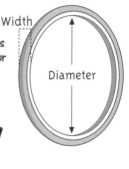

Width

Diameter

WHICH BIKES CAN USE WHICH SIZES

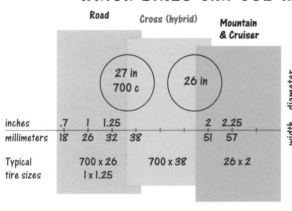

Road

Cross (hybrid)

Mountain & Cruiser

27 in 700 c

26 in

inches	.7	1	1.25		2	2.25
millimeters	18	26	32	38	51	57

Typical tire sizes: 700 x 26 1 x 1.25   700 x 38   26 x 2

width diameter

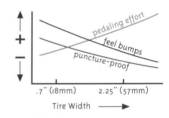

pedaling effort
feel bumps
puncture-proof

.7" (18mm)   2.25" (57mm)

Tire Width ➡

Wider tires:
➤ You feel bumps less
➤ Don't puncture as easily
➤ Make you pedal harder
➤ Recommended if you weigh more than 150 lbs.

PUTTING ON A WIDER TIRE

What if you want wider tires on your bike? The rims of your wheels can probably hold tires that are slightly wider than the ones that came with your bike. For example, if your tire's size is 700 x 28, you can probably use 700 x 32 tires. To learn how wide a tire you can use, show one of your wheels to a bike dealer.

If you install a wider tire and it rubs against the frame no matter how you adjust it, it's too wide.

A wider tire might require you to move the brake pads—otherwise they'll rub the tire instead of the rim.

Which tread should you get?

Feature	Treads		
	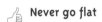 Deep or knobby	Light or semi-slick	Slick
For riding often on dirt or packed snow	X		
Don't turn as easily	X		
Ride on both pavement and dirt		X	
Move faster on pavement			X
Fewer flats	X		

AIRLESS TIRES

WHY & WHY NOT

👍 Never go flat

👍 Never need inflation

👍 Can last several times as long as standard tires

👍 Available in all sizes

👎 Require special tool to install

👎 Cost the same as tire and tube, but you pay all at once

Recommended Product
Nu-Teck Airless Bike Tires
Available in most sizes.
Have your bike dealer order
from Nu-Teck, listed under "Tires"
in Appendix B. (For more on Mr.
Bike's Recommended Products, go
to www.mrbike.com/products.)

BIKE STORAGE

STOP
HERE
AND
READ

You'll use your bike more often if it's convenient. How to make it so? First, make it easy to get your bike in and out of your home. Second, if you don't have much room, look at ways to hang your bike from a wall or ceiling or keep it outdoors. Last, arrange your space so changing clothes isn't a hassle.

Bike-storage hooks
Vinyl-coated hooks screw into wall or ceiling studs.

Changing Area
➤ Dresser or shelves in which to keep clothes and accessories
➤ Hooks on which to hang clothes
➤ Rug on which to change when you're dripping and to put wet shoes
➤ If it's a dark spot, mount a battery-operated wall light

Storage beam
Floor-to-ceiling pole holds up to four bikes. Spring-loaded, so makes no holes in the ceiling or floor.

Easy in and out
In a storage area, rearrange your stuff so the bike goes in and out easily.

Outdoor storage
If you've no room indoors, keep your bike outside. To avoid theft, use an ugly bike (see page 36) and cross-lock to something firm and unmovable, like a metal (not wooden) railing (see page 46).

Stairs
If stairs give you a hassle, nail or tie a board to one side so you can roll your bike. Have a problem with low ceilings on stairways? See page 166.

MAINTENANCE

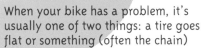

When your bike has a problem, it's usually one of two things: a tire goes flat or something (often the chain) squeaks. If you want to keep your bike running, you should know what to do about these problems.

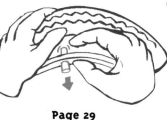

Page 29

You can easily patch a flat or oil a chain once you've seen it done. This chapter shows you how.

What should you do about other problems? First, you should know how to figure out whether your bike even *has* a problem. This chapter shows you **how to check your bike, quick, each time you ride**. This way, you can find little problems before they become big ones.

Page 26

When you don't have the time, tools or know-how, you turn to the **bike shop**. But first you've got to **find one with a good mechanic**. How do you tell the expert from the inept? Find out in this chapter.

Page 27

But maybe you want to **learn to do most repairs yourself**. If so, you'll need some tips to get started. Read 'em here.

Page 30

MAINTENANCE

I f you haven't used your bike in a while, you should check a few things before riding. And even if you use your bike every day, it can get out of whack pretty quickly. These pages tell you how to catch the obvious problems before you ride.

STOP HERE AND READ

Inflation

Tires lose a little air every day. Use a pressure gauge to make sure the tire's pressure isn't more than five pounds under the needed pressure (printed on the side of the tire).

What to do
Add air.

No gauge? Push each tire hard against a curb. If you can flatten it, add air.

Wheel spin

Lift each wheel up and give it a slow spin. (Spin the back wheel forward so the pedals don't move.) Check that it doesn't rub against the brake pads, frame, or anything else.

What to do

1. If the wheel rubs against the frame or the brake pads, loosen the axle nuts or quick-release lever, push the tire so it doesn't rub, and tighten the axle.

2. If the wheel rubs against a brake pad and step 1 doesn't work, move the pads farther from the wheel. You can usually do this by turning an adjuster barrel located at one end of the brake cable. If it still rubs, have a mechanic true the wheel.

3. If the wheel doesn't spin freely but it's not rubbing, have a mechanic check the axle and/or replace the bearings.

Chain

Use your hand to pedal the chain backward.

What to do
It it squeaks or hangs up, lubricate it. If it's badly rusted, have it replaced or have the rust removed.

QUICK CHECK

Tires

Turn each wheel slowly. Look for glass or debris embedded in the tire, and for big cuts.

What to do
Remove glass or other debris. (A small screwdriver helps.) If you spot any big cuts, bulges, bubbles, or places you can see the inner casing, replace the tire.

If the valve stem doesn't point straight at the middle of the wheel, the rim might cut it.

What to do
Let the air out and straighten the valve.

Handlebars

Hold the front tire between your legs and try to turn the handlebars with moderate pressure.

What to do
If the handlebars are loose, tighten the stem bolt slightly.

Shifting

At the start of your ride, try all the gears, shifting each gear lever from high to low. You have a problem if the lever sticks, you can't shift to all gears, the chain rubs the derailleur, or the chain jumps off the gears.

Chain rubs the derailleur

Chain jumps off the gears

What to do
Have a mechanic clean and adjust the derailleur, or replace the derailleur cable and/or housing.

Brakes
Check for any of these problems on each wheel:

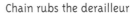

When you apply the brake, one or both brake pads don't touch the rim.

You can squeeze your brake lever all the way to the handlebars.

The brake can't stop the tire from moving on dry, clean pavement.

What to do

1 Try moving the brake pads closer to the wheel. You can usually do this by turning an adjuster barrel, located at one end of the brake cable.

2 If adjustment doesn't work, have a mechanic check the brakes, replacing the brake cables or pads if needed.

FIXING &

How to patch a flat tire

WHAT YOU'LL NEED

➤ Tire patches ➤ Patch glue
➤ Sandpaper or sanding pad ➤ Air pump
➤ Two tire levers or flat-head screwdrivers

Remove

1 Lay your bike on its side or stand it upside down.

2 Use a tire lever or screwdriver to pry the tire over the rim. (Take care with screwdrivers. They can easily puncture your tube.)

3 Leave the lever or screwdriver between the tire and rim so it doesn't pop back in. If you don't have another lever or screwdriver, insert a flat stick.

4 A few inches away, pry out more of the tire. Pry around the tire until you've pried out the entire side.

5 Reach under the tire and pull out the inner tube. Work around the tire until you've pulled the whole tube out.

6 To get the valve out of the rim, hold the tire away from the valve with your thumb. Use your other hand to pull out the valve.

Find

7 Pump air into the tube until it's stretched tight. If you can't find the hole by listening, lightly grab the tube with a circle made by your thumb and fingers. Run your hand around the tube until you feel a stream of air.

8 If you hear but can't see the hole, rub saliva over it. It'll bubble over the hole. If the hole's too big to patch (bigger than a pin-hole) or it's right next to the valve stem, you must remove the wheel and replace the tube.

9 Mark the hole with pen, pencil, stone, or chalk. Draw an asterisk, using the hole as the middle.

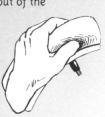

Flat tires are a cyclist's most common problem. If you use your bike a lot, you should know how to patch a flat. But you'll have to fix fewer flats if you take preventive steps (shown on page 31).

STOP HERE AND READ

STOPPING FLATS

Patch

10 Let all the air out of the tube by pushing in the valve stem.

11 Using sandpaper, a metal sanding pad, or a rough stone, roughen the tube around the hole. Roughen an area about as big as a quarter.

12 Squeeze a little glue out of the glue container. Using the container's nozzle, smear the glue over the roughened area.

13 To keep the glue in the tube from drying out: Squeeze the container until glue starts coming out, then cap it.

14 Taking care not to touch the glue, hold the tube against the tire to find where the puncture occurred. Look closely at the tire's outside, and run your fingers along the underside. Remove any debris.

15 Wait till the glue on the tube feels tacky. Remove the foil back from a patch and place onto the glued area. Use a tire lever or coin to smooth the patch down, pressing air bubbles out from the middle. Press with your fingers for about a minute. Then let dry for five more minutes.

Replace

16 Put the valve into its rim hole: On the side of the tire sticking over the rim, hold the tire back with your thumb. Push the valve in, and pull it through on the other side.

17 Pump a little air into the tube to give it shape. Work the tube into the tire, all the way around. Don't let the tube get twisted. If you get to the end and there's too much tube left: Pull the tube out and start over, putting in a little slack as you go.

18 Using your thumbs, push the tire back inside the rim. Don't pinch the tube between the rim and the tire. If the last part won't go over the rim easily, use a tire lever or screwdriver to pry it.

19 Push the valve most of the way into the tire. Make sure the tire sits in the rim evenly. Then pull the valve back out.

Inflate

20 Pump air into the tire until it's inflated, but not hard. Then let all the air out of the tire. This gets the kinks out of the tube.

21 Inflate the tire to its recommended pressure.

Other stuff you need

Air pumps

➤ When using a gas-station pump, fill the tire with short bursts. After each burst, check the air pressure so you don't explode the tire.

➤ Get a floor pump with a built-in pressure gauge. It'll help you keep your tires inflated to the right pressure.

Old sock

Keep an old sock in your bike bag. When you have to make back-wheel repairs, cover one hand with the sock before grabbing your chain. You can also keep your tire patch stuff in the sock.

Bike lock

Always carry a lock so you can lock your bike outside. If your bike breaks down and you don't have time or tools to fix it, you can lock it and get it later. (What kind of lock? See Chapter 3.)

Self-adhesive patches

Self-adhesive patches need no glue: You just peel and stick 'em on. So they're great to have in freezing weather, or at any time your tire-patch glue has dried out.

Danger:
Most of these patches leak after the tire's been deflated.

Smart Idea
Always carry a spare inner tube. Why? You might get a flat and discover you're out of patches or glue. Also, it's hard to patch a flat in extreme cold.

I teach people to learn to fix flats by having them first put on a spare tube—quick and easy. Then I teach them to put on patches.
Cynthia McArthur
fixes bikes in Minneapolis MN

How to remove a wheel

1 Lay the bike on its side or stand it upside down.

2 Loosen the brakes. On some bikes you do this with a lever, on others by turning the barrel adjustor (see page 27).

3 Loosen the axle. On some bikes you flip the quick-release lever. With no quick release, use an adjustable wrench to unscrew the nut on each side of the axle.

4 On a back wheel, pull the derailleur back and hold it. Then pull the wheel out of the frame. Use your hand to free gears from the chain.

5 On a front wheel, remove retainer clips, if present. Then pull the wheel out. To learn how to replace the wheel, see page 18.

Preventing flats

Tactic	How it works	Why	Why not
Tire inflated to maximum air pressure	➤ Repels sharp objects ➤ On hard bumps, tube won't get pinched	Little or no cost	Must do it every week
Kevlar-belted tires	Embedded object can't get thru belt to puncture tube	As easy to install as standard tire	➤ Higher cost ➤ Not 100% effective
Wide tire	Less pressure directed at any single point	As easy to install as standard tire	Takes more effort to ride
Puncture-proof tire liners	Goes between tire and tube to block sharp objects	Effective	Installation slightly tricky (see below)
Thorn-resistant tubes	Thicker and heavier than regular tubes	As easy to install as standard tube	More expensive
Self-sealing tube	Contains liquid sealant that automatically plugs holes	Effective	➤ More expensive ➤ Won't prevent blow-outs ➤ Can clog air valve
Airless tires	Completely solid, no inner tube	Completely eliminates flats	➤ Can't make easier to ride by changing inflation ➤ Tricky to install
Switch front and back tires	Back tire wears faster, so it lasts longer when switched	No cost	It's a hassle

Tire liners

Where the ends of a tire liner overlap, they sometimes chafe the inner tube and cause a flat. You can prevent this by sanding down the ends to make them thinner.

Thorns

In the autumn in much of North America, thorns cause lots of flats. The thorns often come from a plant called the puncture vine *(Tribulus terrestris),* shown here. Watch out for them when you ride on sidewalks or through parking lots. If you ride over some, stop and brush them off your tires. And when one sticks into a tire, some cyclists leave it in. That lets the tire stay inflated long enough to get someplace where they can fix a flat.

LUBRICATION

Choosing a chain lube

Situation	Lube Type	Active Ingredients	Why & Why Not
Clean, dry urban riding	Standard bike lube	Teflon, PTFE, synthetic oil	➤ Penetrates to chain's rollers ➤ Lasts longer than non-bike lubes ➤ Doesn't attract dirt ➤ Relatively inexpensive
	Silicone spray	Silicone	➤ Cheap and doesn't attract dirt ➤ Doesn't last long
	Household oil	Petroleum	➤ Cheap ➤ Attracts dirt, doesn't last long
Ride in rain & fog	Standard bike lube	Teflon, PTFE, synthetic oil	See above
Ride in snow & salt	High-viscosity or long-distance bike lube	Teflon, PAO, molybdenum, detergent polymers	➤ Long-lasting ➤ Attracts less dirt
	Motor oil	Petroleum	➤ Heavy weight (90W) lasts longer ➤ Attracts lots of dirt
Ride in dry dirt & dust	Protective or self-cleaning bike lubes	Paraffin wax	Flake-off film repels dirt

Smart Ideas

➤ Should you get a squeeze bottle or spray? A squeeze bottle drips on, so you waste less lube. But a spray's faster to use.

➤ If a chain's heavily rusted, first try lubing it with a high-penetrating lube. If the chain still squeaks or jerks, remove rust with naval jelly or replace the chain.

➤ Before you lube a chain after riding in wet conditions, spray it with WD-40 to drive out moisture. After WD-40, wipe off the chain and let it dry before lubing.

How to lube a chain

1 Grab the bottom of the chain loosely with a lint-free rag. With the other hand turn the pedals backward, sliding the chain through the rag. Pedal the chain around twice to remove grime.

2 With one hand, pedal the chain backward so it goes completely around once. At the same time, with the other hand drip or spray lubricant onto the chain. **Drip:** Turn the chain slowly and put one drop on each place where two chain links meet. **Spray:** Cover the wheel with a rag so you don't get lube on it. Turn the chain more quickly than for dripping.

3 If you use a lube that can attract dirt (see the table above), repeat step #1 to get the excess lubricant off the chain.

Lubing other parts

What lube to use

Use any general-purpose lubricant. In most cases, household oil works fine. Except for gears, pedals, and axles, lubricate each part once for every 60 days you use your bike. Lube more if you ride in rain or snow.

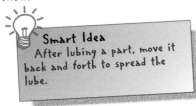

Smart Idea
After lubing a part, move it back and forth to spread the lube.

STOP HERE AND READ

What to do about dry or squeaky parts? It's one of the most common bike problems, especially with chains. It's also the easiest to fix, by lubricating—also known as lubing or oiling. These pages tell you what lubes to use, and how and where.

Back gear assembly (freewheel)
If your back wheel clicks or hums loudly when you coast, lay the bike on its side and drip lube into the hub of the gears. Leave the bike on its side for a while so the lube can work in. If noise persists, replace the assembly.

Brake & derailleur cables
If you ride often in rain or snow, drip lube into the top openings of cable housings. *Don't* do this to self-lubing cables or Teflon housings.

Brakes
Lube where the brake arms connect to the frame and each other.

Gear-shift levers
Lube the pivot points. With hand-grip shifters, lay the bike on its side and drip lube into the place where the shifter meets the handlebars.

Brake levers
Lube the pivot points.

Front derailleur
Lube the hinges.

Back derailleur
Lube the hinges and the gear hubs.

Wheel axles, pedal axle (bottom bracket)
Have a mechanic grease and replace the bearings every year.

Pedals
If a pedal squeaks, lay the bike on its side and drip lube into the pedal's axle. Leave the bike on its side for a while so the lube can work in. If squeaking persists, replace the pedal.

GETTING HELP

Finding a bike shop

One of the best ways to get good, regular maintenance is to find a good bike shop. How? Here are some tips.

1 Ask around. Find people who ride like you do, and are happy with the work done on their bikes. Get the name of their bike shop.

2 Go to a recommended shop and talk with the owner or manager. (If you can, do this when they're not busy: during cold or rainy seasons, or mid-morning on a business day.) Tell them you want to find a shop where you can regularly have your bike fixed.

3 Ask about the mechanics. Are they experienced urban bikers? Also ask if you can use the same mechanic every time (just as you'd always have the same person cut your hair). Some shops hire certain mechanics just for the summer, so you don't know if they'll be around next year.

4 How does the dealer react to your questions? If they seem willing to spend time with you, you might have found a winner.

Do it yourself

Maybe you'd like to know enough about repairs to keep you bike going in emergencies. Or maybe you can't pay a bike shop every time you need repairs. If so, learn to fix stuff yourself—it's easier than you might think! Several ways to learn:

➤ Take a class. Many bike dealers, community colleges, and bike clubs offer bike-repair classes.

➤ Get a book. Some books on fixing bikes are easy to follow. Find one you like at a bookstore or bike shop. Appendix A lists some popular bike-maintenance books.

➤ Get an advisor. Find a friend or bike dealer who's willing to advise you when you can't figure stuff out. In exchange for a bike dealer's help with your bike, you can:

1 Buy the tools and parts you need at their shop.

2 Refer your friends to them.

3 Put off big repairs until cold or rainy months, when they need business.

AVOIDING RIP-OFF

Lots of bikes get ripped off because people park them in the wrong places. A good lock is a bad joke if a thief saws through the fence it's locked to. In this chapter you'll **learn the good and bad places to lock** your bike.

Page 47

Some locks have been around so long that thieves treat them like pet dogs: they take them out every day. **Which ones do thieves know best?** This chapter tells you.

Page 55

It's not only locks that turn thieves away. If you **make your bike look ugly**, you might steer a thief toward somebody else's bike that looks better. This chapter tells you how.

Page 38

But, in spite of good locking, what if your bike finally does get ripped off? There's one good way to prepare: Give your bike I.D. If someone finds your stolen bike, **positive I.D. helps get it back to you**. This chapter describes a bunch of different ways to I.D.

Also, many stolen bikes don't go far from where they got snatched. Knowing where to look can **help you find your stolen bike**. You'll get ideas on where to look from this chapter.

Page 42

How to Uglify

Wrap the frame with inner tubes or tape

STOP HERE AND READ

Many thieves can't tell a cheap bike from a titanium-alloy wallet buster. They simply go for anything that looks new and shiny. So how do you keep thieves from looking at your bike, whether it's a Kmart special or a high-tech ultra-light? Uglify!

If your handlebars have bright tape, cover them with black tape.

Cut inner tubes open, and wrap long strips around frame.

Wrap tight next to cables so they don't rub too much.

Use separate pieces to get around water bottle cages.

Cover every possible part of the frame with your materials.

WHY & WHY NOT

👍 You can remove the ugly covering later.

👎 Might interfere with your cables.

YOUR BIKE

Paint your frame and cover it with stickers

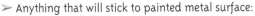

WHAT YOU'LL NEED

➤ Anything that will stick to painted metal surface:

➤ Tape
➤ Nail polish
➤ Oil-based paint

➤ Bumper or fruit stickers
➤ Laundry marker

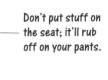

Don't put stuff on
the seat; it'll rub
off on your pants.

Whenever you eat a banana,
take the label and stick it on
your bike.

Use dark colors for a
more repulsive effect.

Avoid moving parts.

WHY & WHY NOT

👍 The ugliness you can achieve
is limited only by your
imagination.

👎 If you want to remove this stuff
later, it'll take lots of work.

Before uglifying

Ride a junky-looking used bike

WHY & WHY NOT

👍 Takes little effort.

👎 Costs money.

Smart Idea
Don't buy a bike off the street; it's probably stolen. You might get a good deal, but you'll support the work of thieves.

Take the bike to a bike dealer and get it fixed up.

Buy an old used bike at a garage sale, or take an old bike of your own.

Replace tires, cables, and bearings.

Clean and lube the chain and brakes.

Let your bike get dirty

When your bike gets dirty from riding in rain, snow, or mud, clean off the moving parts only.

Let dirt stay on the frame and tires.

WHY & WHY NOT

👍 Takes little effort.

👎 Dirt comes off on your clothes and hands.

Smart Idea
New tires can make a bike look new! Get new tires with dark sidewalls, or used tires.

I.D.ING YOUR BIKE
PRE-THEFT

Hiding I.D. inside your bike

WHY & WHY NOT

👍 To make it easier to I.D. your bike at an auction or pawn shop.

👍 Thieves can't see it, so it will remain where you put it.

How to hide I.D.

1 Take several 3-by-2-inch pieces of light cardboard. On them write your name, address, and phone number. Or use your business card. Write on it, "If you find this card, this bike was stolen from me."

2 Remove the cap or hand grip from one end of your handlebars. Curl up one card and slide it in.

3 Put the other card into a small plastic bag and seal it with tape to keep it dry. Remove your seat from the seat post. Curl up the bagged card and slide it in. Use a pencil to push it down. (To remove it, use a straightened-out coat hanger with a hooked end.)

seat post tube

4 Put another card between your tire and inner tube. When your stolen bike's new owner fixes a flat (the most common repair), they might contact you.

Registering your bike

How to find a registry

City or state registration
Ask your local bike dealer if your city or state has a program for registering bikes. If it does, ask how to register.

Private registries
Several private organizations run national bike registries. For contact info, see "Registries, national" in Appendix B.

In every city, police recover hundreds of stolen bikes each year but can't find their owners. But if your bike's registered, police can get it back to you.

STOP HERE AND READ

Where to find your serial number

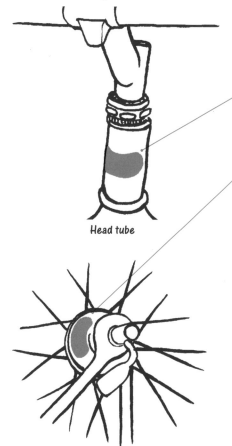

Head tube

PRIVATE REGISTRIES: WHY & WHY NOT

👍 Available even if your city or state doesn't have a registration program.

👍 Lets police in other areas identify you as the owner of a recovered bike.

👎 The programs mark your bike with a decal that a thief can cover or remove.

👎 Not all police know about the private registries. So the registries don't help if the decal's removed and police who recover your bike don't know to call the registry.

Rear wheel mount

How to register

Bike registrations are just like the ones for cars: they describe the make, model, color, and serial number. Keep a copy of this information for yourself.

1 Find your bike's serial number.

2 Fill out the registration form and send it in.

3 If the registration uses a decal, clean a spot on the seat post tube and stick it there.

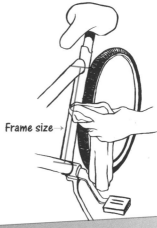

Frame size→

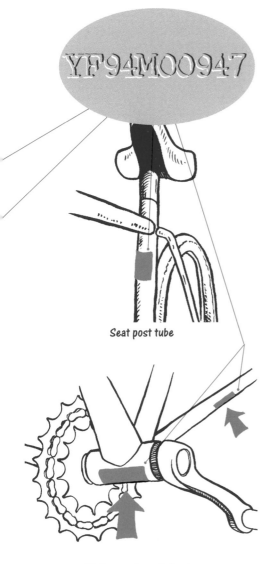

YF94M00947

Seat post tube

Under crank or chain stay

Smart Ideas

➤ If your bike has more than one series of numbers stamped onto the frame, it's hard to know which is the serial number. So write them all down.

➤ If your town doesn't register bikes, find a bike-riding cop and put him or her in touch with a national bike registry.

Etching your bike

WHAT YOU'LL NEED

➤ Electric engraving tool   ➤ Stamping tools

or

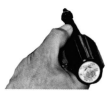

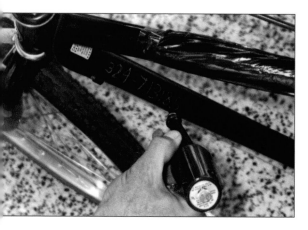

> **Smart Idea**
> Have someone take a
> photograph of you standing
> next to your bike. This way,
> if a thief somehow erases
> etched numbers on your
> bike, you'll have another
> way to prove the bike's
> yours.

How to engrave

1 Pick an obvious place on your bike's frame, like the top of the top tube.

2 Engrave your social security or social insurance number. If you want to make it easier for police to find you, etch your telephone number and first name.

3 To prevent rust, cover the etched area with clear fingernail polish or spray lacquer.

WHY & WHY NOT

👍 It's hard for thieves to sell stolen **goods that have etched I.D. Unless a thief wants the trouble of covering or filing down an etch, he'll take a different bike.**

👍 **You can more easily I.D. your bike at an auction or pawn shop.**

👍 Registering your bike isn't **enough. When you engrave, if someone other than a cop finds your bike, they can find you.**

👍 **Thieves sometimes** remove a bike's serial number.

Insuring your bike

Lock manufacturers

If you can prove a lock failed, some lock manufacturers will reimburse you for a stolen bike. Usually you must first register your bike. See the theft agreement that came with your lock. The sample agreements shown here tell you what to look for.

WHY & WHY NOT

 If thieves steal your expensive bike, insurance will help pay for a new one.

 Some plans have extensive limitations.

Protection in the first year often free; sometimes you can pay for extra years.

No payout if you don't return the broken lock.

No payout if you don't return all the keys.

UNCONDITIONAL LIFETIME WARRANTY

We warrant this product to be free from defects in materials and workmanship under normal use for the life of the product. If this product contains a defect in materials or workmanship, we will replace it for free. Just send the defective lock to Sisko Lock Company, 418 9th Street, Bajor DS 90009, USA. We'll send you a new lock and a check to cover your postage. You do not have to send a receipt.

LIMITED ANTI-THEFT AGREEMENT

If theft of your bicycle is due to the Sisko product being broken or opened by forceful means, Sisko will pay you the value of your bicycle up to $US 4,000, subject to the limitations and conditions described below (the "Limited Anti-Theft Agreement"). This Limited Anti-Theft Agreement applies, at no additional cost, to the original consumer purchaser only for one (1) year following the purchase of your Sisko product as shown on your original sales receipt. (The original buyer may extend the Agreement for two (2) additional years for an added fee as described below.) This Limited Anti-Theft Agreement is not to be construed as insurance.

REGISTRATION CONDITIONS

To validate this Limited Anti-Theft Agreement:
1. Mail, by certified mail, to Sisko Lock Co., 418 9th Street, Bajor DS 90009, USA, the following items within 15 days of purchase of your Sisko lock:
   a. A completed registration form that came with your lock.
   b. The original sales receipt for the purchase of your lock.
   c. The original UPC bar code label from the Sisko package (we will not accept photocopies).
   d. A copy of the sales receipt from the purchase of your bicycle or, if not available, a signed and dated appraisal for your bicycle from your dealer on the dealer's letterhead.
2. Register your bicycle with an official authority (your local police department or other appropriate agency) unless such registration is unavailable. Identify the agency you registered with in the space provided on the agreement registr...

IN THE EVENT OF A THEFT
A. Report the theft to the police within 72 hours.
B. Notify Defiant within seven (7) days by certified mail to Defiant Lock Co., 2 Sao Paulo Pl., Dockport NX 74205, USA, and include:
   1. A copy of the police report showing that you reported the theft to police within 72 hours of discovery of the theft. Failure to report theft to police within 72 hours voids this agreement.
   2. A copy of the claim filed with your insurance company, if covered.
   3. Your broken Defiant lock.
   4. All original keys from your Defiant product (unless you purchased a combination lock). Failure to return all keys voids this agreement.

LIMITATIONS
A. Defiant will not be liable if theft occurred because:
   1. The frame of the bicycle was not properly locked to a solidly anchored, immovable object.
   2. The object to which the bicycle was locked was dismantled or cut.
   3. The lock was opened by means of a torch, battery-operated tool, or power tool.
B. Defiant's total liability under the terms of this Guarantee is limited to:
   1. The purchase price of the stolen bicycle including manufacturer's original equipment and excluding separately purchased accessories or taxes, up to $4,000.
   2. The amount of item (1) above less the amount of any other insurance collectible due to the theft.
   3. The replacement cost of the bicycle only, and not any damages connected with an attempted theft.
C. This Guarantee does not cover bicycles used commercially and applies only to thefts occurring in the 50 United States of America, District of Columbia, Canada and Puerto Rico.
D. The maximum amount we'll pay to any owner is $4,000 in U.S. currency regardless of the number and kind of bicycles registered under this Guarantee.
E. If your address is in the State of New York, or if the receipt for your Defiant product shows it was purchased in the State of New York, you will receive up to $4,000 of insurance protection instead of Defiant's Agreement. This insurance remains in force for (1) year from the date of purchase and is not renewable. If your bicycle is stolen your rights and obligations will be those set forth in the certifi-cate of insurance that you will receive rather than...

No payout if the locked-to object is cut.

No payout if the thief uses a torch or power tool.

Registering the lock might include getting your bike appraised, keeping the bar code from the lock package, having proof of police bike registration, and sending all this stuff by certified mail.

Protection for only one year in New York State.

Home or apartment insurers

If you have homeowner's or renter's insurance, ask your agent how to insure your bike. Also, some companies insure personal property (such as bikes) without renter's or homeowner's insurance. In any case, make sure the bike's covered whether it's stolen inside or outside your home.

What to do after it's stolen

1 Save remaining parts
Look around on the ground for leftover parts of your lock or bike. You might need them later to show to the police or lock manufacturer.

2 Find serial number
Find your bike's serial number and, if you have it, a copy of your registration. If you don't have the serial number, try getting it from the store where you bought the bike.

3 Report to police & registry
➤ Report the theft to the police in the town in which your bike was stolen.
➤ Ask for a police report number.
➤ Ask police how they'll contact you if they find your bike.
➤ If the bike's listed with a private registry, contact the registry.

4 If your bike's insured
Report the theft to your insurance company or lock manufacturer.

Smart Ideas
➤ If you find your bike, lock it with your own lock. That way, it won't go anywhere until you can persuade the current owner to give it up.
➤ If you find a junk shop selling lots of bikes, they're probably stolen. Tell your local bike clubs, advocacy group, or city bike agency. They can spread the word to other cyclists.

If you find your stolen bike

1 Finding your bike means zip unless you can prove it's yours. Make sure you have a copy of your serial number, or can otherwise prove the bike's yours. (See "I.D.ing your bike" on page 39.)

2 Tell the seller the bike belongs to you, and show them your serial number or other identification. Then match your I.D. to the one on your bike.

3 If the seller refuses to give you the bike, leave—then return with the police.

YOUR STOLEN BIKE

Where to look for your bike

Flea markets

Junk shops or pawn shops
If you don't see bikes on display, ask if they have any.

"For sale" ads in newspapers Look within the first two weeks of your theft.

Police auctions
Police recover many stolen bikes. Ask your local police when they hold auctions.

Offering a reward

➤ Stick your reward flyer to lampposts and sign poles in the neighborhood in which your bike was stolen.

➤ If your town has bike messengers, send a reward flyer to each messenger company.

I put up flyers all over the neighborhood, offering a $100 reward for my bike. I got it back in three days.

Patti Howells, San Francisco
on offering rewards

WHERE TO PARK

Some thieves don't steal bikes where lots of people are walking around. But if you park next to a bunch of other bikes, you give a thief cover: while he's stealing your bike, he looks like just another cyclist. So park away from other bikes but out in the open, where people pass very close to the bike.

If you're parking your bike and a car passes you several times, watch out. If the occupants keep looking at you, they're probably planning to steal your bike. Move to another spot.

STOP HERE AND READ

When you arrive at your destination, or even at home, where do you park your bike? How you choose a parking place can cut your chances of rip-off.

Some cities and businesses provide thick metal bike racks embedded into the sidewalk. These are secure places to park.

Some public parking lots will let you park your bike for a small fee. If you forget your lock, look for an attended parking lot.

YOUR BIKE

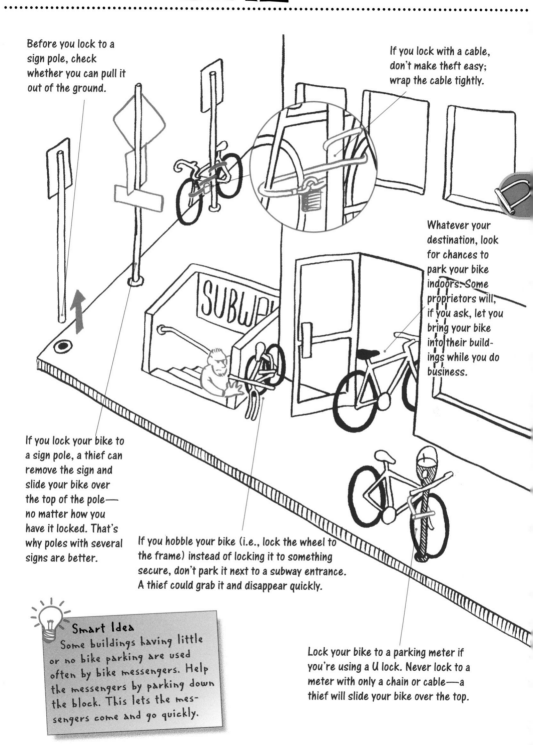

Before you lock to a sign pole, check whether you can pull it out of the ground.

If you lock with a cable, don't make theft easy; wrap the cable tightly.

Whatever your destination, look for chances to park your bike indoors. Some proprietors will, if you ask, let you bring your bike into their buildings while you do business.

If you lock your bike to a sign pole, a thief can remove the sign and slide your bike over the top of the pole— no matter how you have it locked. That's why poles with several signs are better.

If you hobble your bike (i.e., lock the wheel to the frame) instead of locking it to something secure, don't park it next to a subway entrance. A thief could grab it and disappear quickly.

Smart Idea
Some buildings having little or no bike parking are used often by bike messengers. Help the messengers by parking down the block. This lets the messengers come and go quickly.

Lock your bike to a parking meter if you're using a U lock. Never lock to a meter with only a chain or cable—a thief will slide your bike over the top.

How to Lock

Always lock

Never, never leave your bike unlocked—even if you leave it for only half a minute. A thief can grab your bike in seconds.

Lock to fixed objects

Lock your bike to something that's permanent and not easy for a thief to take. Don't lock to another bike, a door handle, a wooden fence post, or a small tree. (See pages 46–47.)

(See pages 46–47.)

STOP HERE AND READ

You need good, reliable locks to stop thieves from stealing your bike. But the way you lock is just as important.

Parts: tie 'em

Get a 12-inch piece of old bike chain. Put it through the metal runners on the underside of your seat. Have a mechanic help you join the ends of the chain.

Chain link fences

Always lock to the metal posts of chain link fences, not the links. To get your bike close enough, hang one handlebar over the top of the fence.

Lock the whole bike

Put your chain, cable, or U locks through your frame and both wheels.

Parts: take 'em

Remove any parts you can't lock and a thief could grab easily: a quick-release seat, horn, bike bag, pump, water bottle, or lights. If removing quick-release parts is a hassle, replace them with permanent ones.

Wheelize

Never lock through your wheel without locking the frame. Even if you don't have quick-release wheels, a thief can unbolt your wheel in seconds.

Take the front wheel off, if you have to. (This is easier with quick-release wheels.)

URBAN BIKERS' TRICKS & TIPS

Cross lock

Because most people only use one lock, you should use two. That way, a thief will go for somebody else's bike. (For more info, see page 53.)

GOOD

Put one lock through your frame and rear wheel, and put the second through your frame and front wheel.

BETTER

You need one kind of tool to cut a metal bar (such as a lock shackle) and a different tool to cut a metal cable. Most thieves don't carry both. (At least, until they read this.) So a good way to foil thieves is to use both a shackle-type lock, such as a U lock, and a cable with a built-in lock.

Lock in storage

In the U.S., about a fifth of bike thefts occur in residences. If you keep your bike in a garage, basement, or on a porch, lock it.

Parts: seal 'em

Plug the head of your handlebar-release bolt with silicon adhesive, epoxy, or rubber cement so a thief can't unbolt your handlebars. When you need to, remove the plug with a knife.

NO

YES

Locks in space

Thieves can open some locks by hitting them with a hammer. But to break the lock, the lock must be placed against something hard, like a wall or sidewalk. If you use a padlock, wrap your chain or cable tightly, and place the lock so it can't be put up against a hard surface.

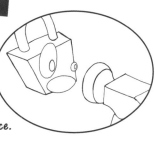

How to MAKE

Beating the Pry

Some locks have the keyhole at the end of the cross bar. Because the cross bar sticks out, a thief can slip the end of a long pipe over it and pry the cross bar off.

W H A T   T O   D O

1 Collar

From a hardware store, get a piece of pipe hardware called a T joint.

Or go to a bike shop and get a U lock collar.

Slip it over the lock's keyhole end.

2 Position

Face the keyhole end toward the sidewalk or a wall so a thief can't get a pipe over it.

I S   Y O U R   L O C K   A B O U T   T O   D I E ?

When your lock gets worn, it can freeze up so that you can't unlock it.

How you know it's ready to die: It starts getting hard for you to turn the key.

W H A T   T O   D O

Every month, squirt oil or some other lube into your keyhole. Do it more often if your bike sits outside frequently, or if you lock it many times per day.

If your lock gets rained on, squirt WD-40 inside the keyhole to drive out moisture.

YOUR U LOCK BETTER

Beating the Pop

If the opening is wide enough, a thief can stick a thick pipe or expanding car-tire jack into the U and pop it open.

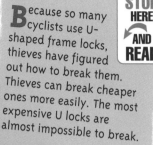

Because so many cyclists use U-shaped frame locks, thieves have figured out how to break them. Thieves can break cheaper ones more easily. The most expensive U locks are almost impossible to break.

STOP HERE AND READ

WHAT TO DO

1 Fill
Lock your bike so the entire middle of the U is filled, leaving no room to stick a tool in. One way to fill it: Lock both of your tires and your frame to a thick metal pole.

2 Straps
Buy steel reinforcement straps that slip onto the U and fill the space. (Have your bike dealer order from Joannou, listed under "Locks & accessories" in Appendix B.)

> ☀ **Smart Idea**
> Get a mini-U lock, or a U lock with a narrow shackle. For examples see page 55.

BEFORE YOU

How much should you spend?

The more you pay for your lock, the better it will protect you.
How much should you spend? If it would cost a lot to replace your
bike, you should invest in a very good lock. Spend less when you have
a cheap bike. Use these charts as a guide:

Bike replacement cost	Spend this much on locks
$100	one-third ($33)
$200	one-fifth ($40)
$300	one-fifth ($60)
$400	one-sixth ($67)

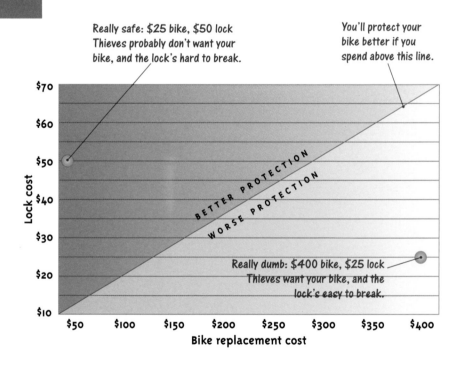

Really safe: $25 bike, $50 lock
Thieves probably don't want your
bike, and the lock's hard to break.

You'll protect your
bike better if you
spend above this line.

BETTER PROTECTION

WORSE PROTECTION

Really dumb: $400 bike, $25 lock
Thieves want your bike, and the
lock's easy to break.

Lock cost

Bike replacement cost

BUY A LOCK

Cross lock: buy two independent systems

Hardware combinations for cross locking

frame lock

heavy chain with thick padlock

> Can weigh lots, but the extra security can be worth it.

frame lock

heavy cable with thick padlock

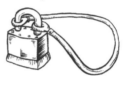

> Careful: Thieves can cut cheap cables easily.

chain with padlock

heavy cable with built-in lock

> Don't get a cheap cable lock; they're easy to pick (more info on page 58).

New Word
Cross locking
When you cross lock your bike, you use two different lock systems at once—such as a U lock and a cable. Cross locking forces thieves to spend more time and use more than one kind of tool. If a thief sees that your bike is cross locked, he might move on to another bike that isn't.

BUYING A NEW

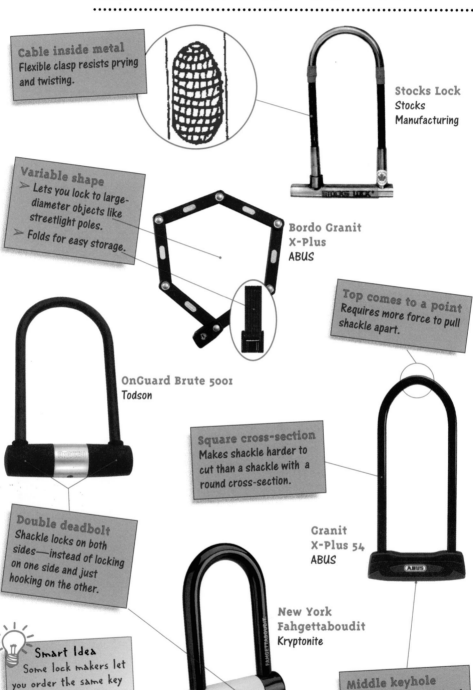

Cable inside metal
Flexible clasp resists prying and twisting.

Stocks Lock
Stocks Manufacturing

Variable shape
➤ Lets you lock to large-diameter objects like streetlight poles.
➤ Folds for easy storage.

Bordo Granit X-Plus
ABUS

Top comes to a point
Requires more force to pull shackle apart.

OnGuard Brute 5001
Todson

Square cross-section
Makes shackle harder to cut than a shackle with a round cross-section.

Double deadbolt
Shackle locks on both sides—instead of locking on one side and just hooking on the other.

Granit X-Plus 54
ABUS

New York Fahgettaboudit
Kryptonite

Smart Idea
Some lock makers let you order the same key for all the locks you own. They call this "locks keyed alike."

Middle keyhole
Keyhole is in the middle of the cross bar so the end doesn't stick out.

FRAME LOCK

Retractable
You can make the inner space smaller so thieves can't pry or pop the lock.

Ultra Bike Club Junior
WInner International

Many bicyclists use a U-shaped type of frame lock—a lock that's big enough to fit around part of a bike's frame and tires. But frame locks come in many types; they're shaped like "U"s, rectangles, and even circles. The expensive ones have different features that make them bad for thieves.

STOP HERE AND READ

OnGuard Brute 5112
Todson

Narrow space
Narrow inner space makes it hard for thieves to get a tool inside to pry or pop the lock open.

WHAT'S WRONG WITH CHEAP U LOCKS

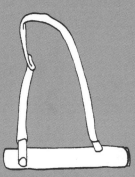

Cheap U locks are easier for thieves to cut, pry open with a lever, or pop with a tire jack.

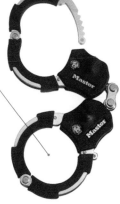

Street Cuff
Master Lock

Force 8196D
Master Lock

Built-in holder
Makes it easy to carry the lock on your bike frame. (If your lock doesn't come with a holder, you can buy one separately.)

New Word
Shackle
On a lock, the piece of metal (usually curved) that inserts into the main body of the lock.

PADLOCKS,

Padlocks

WHAT TO GET

➢ Shackles 3/8 inch (10 mm.) thick or more
➢ Case-hardened shackle

DON'T GET

➢ Combination locks
➢ Shackles less than 5/16 inch (8 mm.) thick

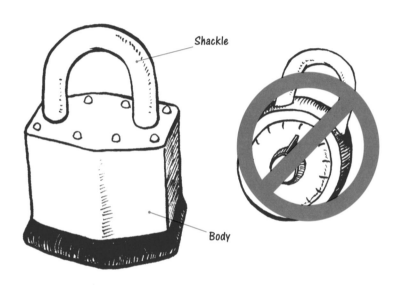

Shackle

Body

> **New Word**
> **Case hardening**
> A piece of metal is case hardened by heating it. Case hardening makes the outside harder, so a thief can't cut it as easily. But case hardening doesn't harden the inside of the metal, so it doesn't become brittle. A thief could break a brittle piece of metal by twisting it.

How to tell if a lock is case hardened:
The words "case hardened" appear on the lock or the package. If these words don't appear, don't believe a salesperson who tells you the lock is case hardened.

CHAINS, & CABLES

Chains

WHAT TO GET

➢ Case-hardened links 3/8 inch (10 mm.) thick or more

➢ Thick chains with four-sided or six-sided links

DON'T GET

➢ Links less than 5/16 inch (8 mm.) thick

How to tell if a chain is case hardened:

LISTEN

If you rattle a case-hardened chain against a hard surface, it'll make a bright, ringing sound. A non-hardened chain will sound duller.

LOOK

If the words "anti-theft" appear on a chain or its package, it's usually case hardened. There's no other way to tell a case-hardened chain by looking at it.

Chains with four-sided or six-sided links

Thieves can't cut chains with links having square or hexagonal cross-sections (like the ones shown below) as easily as they can cut chains with links having round cross-sections.

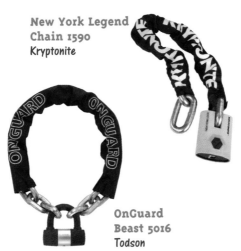

New York Legend Chain 1590
Kryptonite

OnGuard Beast 5016
Todson

QuadraChain
St. Pierre Manufacturing

Wire cables

WHAT TO GET

➤ Cables 3/8 inch (10 mm.) thick or more

➤ Cables with more than 300 strands

DON'T GET

➤ Cables 5/16 inch (8 mm.) thick or less

How cables stop thieves

1 Type of cutter

Bolt cutters can snap hard metal. But they can't snap cable. So if a thief wants to cut both locks and cables, he needs both a bolt cutter and a cable cutter or hacksaw. Most thieves don't carry both.

2 Thick & dense

Cables that stop thieves are either very thick (3/8 inch or more) or very dense. Very dense cables have 300 to 900 strands. Inferior cables have only 100 to 200 strands.

3 Lock

When using a cable, don't use a padlock that has a shackle less than 3/8 inch (10 mm.) thick; a thief can simply cut the lock. (You can also use a cable with a built-in lock—but you shouldn't get a cheap one.)

Where to get wire cables

Most bike stores sell cable that's only 5/16 inch (8 mm.) thick. For thicker cables, you must find a cable supplier. Look in your yellow pages telephone directory under "Cable," "Wire & Cable," "Wire Products," or "Wire Rope."

Recommended Product
Flexweave 9/16" cable
Has over 800 strands.
Have your bike dealer order from Kabletek, listed under "Locks & accessories" in Appendix B. (For more on Mr. Bike's Recommended Products, go to www.mrbike.com/products.)

Armored cables

Armored cables usually have a an inner wire cable covered by steel plates or links. So thieves can find them harder to cut than a simple wire cable.

Outer layer of metal links

Core made of wire cable

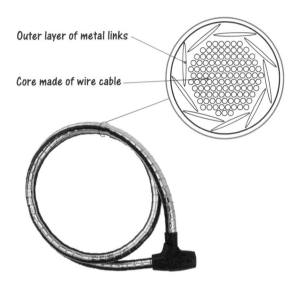

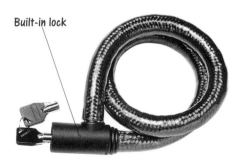

Built-in lock

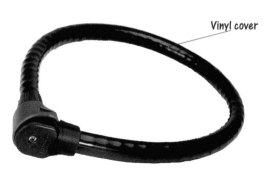

Vinyl cover

Many wire cables have a plastic outer casing. If you can't see through the casing to the metal, measure the width of the casing. Then subtract 1/16 inch (2 mm.). If you can see through the casing, measure only the width of the metal inside.

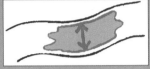

Thickness guide

inches	millimeters
1/4	7
5/16	9
3/8	10
7/16	12
1/2	13
9/16	15
5/8	16

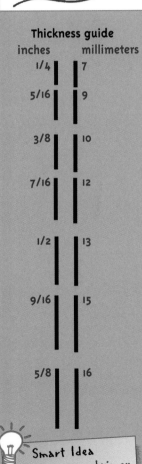

Smart Idea
To carry your chain or cable, wrap it tightly around your seat post, and lock it.

GETTING THROUGH TRAFFIC

4

Sometimes you want to **get some-where more quickly** than usual. Or you think you take too many chances. Or you think: I should be able to **maneuver this bike a lot better** than I move a two-ton car; how can I? This chapter can help you in each case.

Page 103

Page 105

Also, if police in your area are cracking down on cyclists, **you can't just blast through red lights**. This chapter will give you other options. Some are perfectly legal. Others aren't, but at least they're not obvious.

This chapter will also have you **threading through traffic jams, beating red lights, and spotting problems** before they trip you. You can feel all the power of a motor vehicle—with none of the pollution.

Page 104

When you start feeling powerful, it shows. **Motorists notice your confidence and trust you to act like you know what you're doing.** It helps to give them clear gestures too, which this chapter explains.

Page 70

But **what if you're afraid of traffic?** Two things can help: Knowing how cyclists really get hurt, and practice. This chapter tells you about both of these.

Page 115

SLY BIKING

Sly Bikers Only!

To some, getting through traffic fast means brute force: running red lights, cutting off pedestrians, going the wrong way, and breaking traffic laws. Such actions can move you faster, and this chapter shows you the best ways to do some of them—if that's how you want to bicycle.

But you have another option: sly biking. Sly biking means, for example, that you time traffic lights instead of racing to beat them. It means that you *feel* what the motorist ahead of you will do before he or she does it, so you react immediately— without slowing down.

Good dancers glide all over the floor in subtle, complex motions. But they don't step on others' feet or get in others' ways. Likewise, the best sly biker can beat traffic without scaring peds or making motorists hit their brakes.

PED MODE

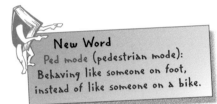
STOP HERE AND READ

In many places, people don't know that bicyclists are supposed to obey traffic laws. In fact, when you're on the street with your bike, you won't surprise most people if you suddenly get off of your bike and start walking. After all, that's one convenience of biking: the ability to suddenly become a pedestrian.

WHY

You can often get through traffic quicker.

Most pedestrians, motorists, and police officers think it's OK for cyclists to act like pedestrians.

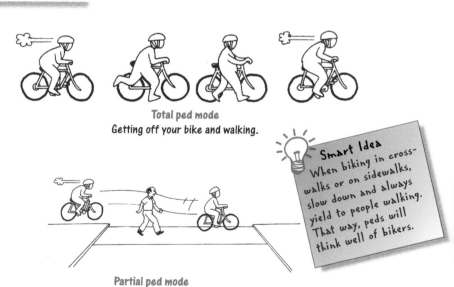

Total ped mode
Getting off your bike and walking.

Smart Idea
When biking in crosswalks or on sidewalks, slow down and always yield to people walking. That way, peds will think well of bikers.

Partial ped mode
Riding your bike in places where people usually walk, like crosswalks and sidewalks.

SURPRISE FACTS

1 NOT AS DANGEROUS AS IT LOOKS

Bicycling in traffic isn't as scary as it looks from the sidewalk. Bicyclists don't usually get hit by motorists from behind— one of the most common fears. Cyclists do get into trouble when they don't act like the other vehicles around them—namely, cars.

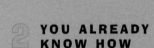

2 YOU ALREADY KNOW HOW

Because you probably know how to drive a car, you already know how to get through traffic. You just have to apply this knowledge to bicycling.

3 YOU'VE ALREADY TAKEN BIGGER RISKS

More bike crashes happen on off-street paths than in traffic. Why? On paths, people bike next to walkers, runners, skaters,

If you don't already ride in traffic, this page has a few tips to help make you more comfortable.

STOP HERE AND READ

How to learn

1 PRACTICE

At first, biking next to two-ton hunks of metal (cars) scares most people. How do you get over it? Walk or drive your bike to a quiet parking lot and ride around. Ride down rows of cars, getting closer and closer. When you get within four feet of a line of cars, practice looking inside the cars. Look for people who might open doors or pull out in front of you. Then practice following cars through the lot. When you're ready, repeat these steps on a quiet side street.

2 GET TO KNOW YOUR BIKE

You might not ever need these skills, but knowing how your bike performs will build your confidence. Learn how small a space your bike will fit through by riding between objects, such as parked cars or sign poles. Do this until you can judge spaces on sight.

COMFORTABLE WITH TRAFFIC

3 TAKE IT EASY

Remember that on a street, you either **share the lane** (cars pass next to you) or **take the lane** (you ride in the middle, and cars stay behind you or pass in another lane). If a street's not wide enough for you to share safely, and taking the lane scares you, stay off that street—at least until you feel more comfortable. Riding behind an experienced partner can help.

4 TAKE A CLASS

Thousands have learned to ride confidently in traffic by taking a Smart Cycling (U.S.) or CAN-BIKE (Canada) class. To find one near you, contact the League of American Bicyclists or Canadian Cycling Association (listed under "National advocacy groups" in Appendix A).

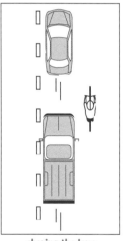
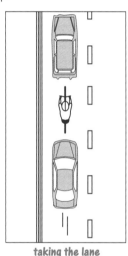

| sharing the lane | taking the lane |

Learn how well your brakes work: go fast, then try to stop within 10 feet. Then try to stop within six feet, then three feet, then one. Also see how quickly you can speed up from a stop. For more info on stopping, see page 146.

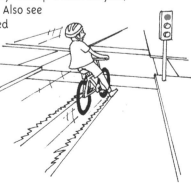

LOOKING

The up-and-down scan

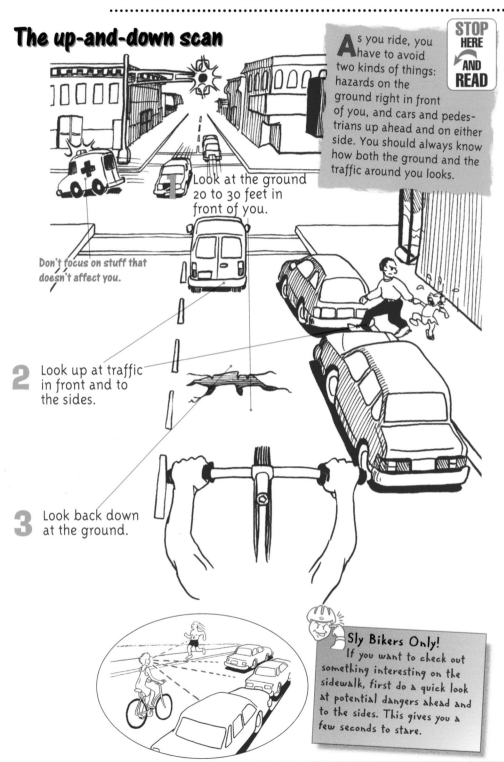

STOP HERE AND READ

As you ride, you have to avoid two kinds of things: hazards on the ground right in front of you, and cars and pedestrians up ahead and on either side. You should always know how both the ground and the traffic around you looks.

1 Look at the ground 20 to 30 feet in front of you.

Don't focus on stuff that doesn't affect you.

2 Look up at traffic in front and to the sides.

3 Look back down at the ground.

Sly Bikers Only!
If you want to check out something interesting on the sidewalk, first do a quick look at potential dangers ahead and to the sides. This gives you a few seconds to stare.

TECHNIQUES

When a vehicle blocks your view

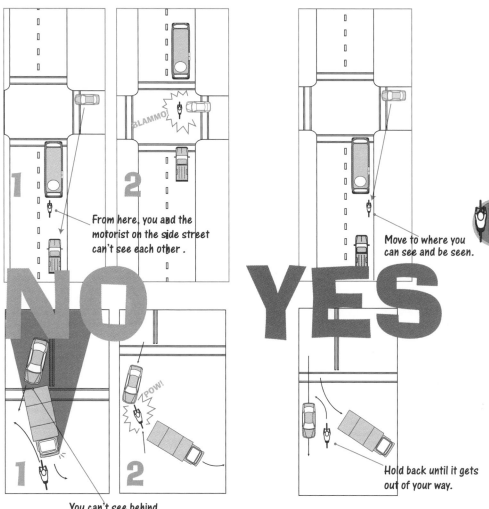

From here, you and the motorist on the side street can't see each other.

NO

YES

Move to where you can see and be seen.

You can't see behind the big vehicle.

POW!

BLAMMO!

Hold back until it gets out of your way.

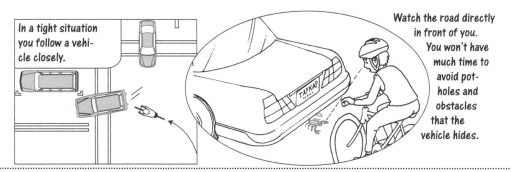

In a tight situation you follow a vehicle closely.

Watch the road directly in front of you. You won't have much time to avoid potholes and obstacles that the vehicle hides.

How to practice looking back

1 Find a parking lot or wide, quiet street with some kind of lane stripe.

2 Ride along the lane stripe in a straight line.

3 Keeping your left shoulder steady and your left arm relaxed, turn your head down and around to the left. Try to steer straight.

4 Turn your head forward.

5 Turn your head back again. Pick out something to look back at. Try to keep moving straight.

STOP HERE AND READ

Looking back over your shoulder helps you move left or right fast—to avoid hazards, change lanes, or make a turn. And looking over your shoulder makes drivers pay attention to you. Even if you have a mirror, you should always turn your head to look before you move left or right—just as you would when driving a car.

8 Next, practice turning your head to the right. Then practice turning your head while moving faster.

7 If you can't turn your head without turning your handlebars, drop your left hand down to your thigh while you turn your head.

6 Turn your head forward.

USING BODY LANGUAGE

Will they yield?

1 When you're not sure a motorist will yield, look at where their eyes are. If they're not looking at you, slow down and prepare to get out of the way.

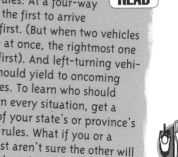

STOP HERE AND READ

As vehicle drivers, both you and motorists should follow right-of-way rules: At a four-way stop, the first to arrive goes first. (But when two vehicles arrive at once, the rightmost one goes first). And left-turning vehicles should yield to oncoming vehicles. To learn who should yield in every situation, get a copy of your state's or province's traffic rules. What if you or a motorist aren't sure the other will yield when they should? Here's what to do.

2 If the motorist or ped is looking at you, watch what they do next. If they don't move toward you, they'll probably yield.

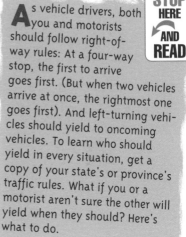

3 To make sure they know what you want, use your hand to say "Wait!" Or "I'm going there."

4 Wave thanks to the motorist or ped who yields.

Motorists at stop signs

COMMUNICATING WITH YOUR HANDS AND HEAD

I'm turning (for observers in front & behind)

I'm slowing
(for observers behind)

I'm going there

Wait!

Go ahead

1 When approaching a cross street with a car stopped at a stop sign, make eye contact with the motorist.

2 If you think the motorist will yield to you, start going through the intersection.

Check for obstacles in your escape routes.

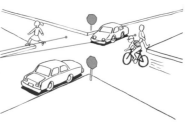
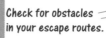

3

If the car suddenly moves to cut you off, make an emergency right turn (see page 147) parallel to the car.

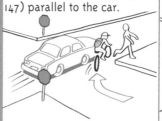

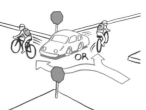

If a car approaches from the right and you have room, curve in front of it.

Danger
Motorists at stop signs who don't yield to cross traffic are one of the top causes of bike crashes!

Oncoming left-turning cars

1 Where an oncoming car has signaled a left turn, you speed up to beat the car to the intersection. (And, to be obvious, you move to the middle of the lane.)

2 Looks like you've beat the car. But:

Even if you want to slow down, don't stop pedaling; the motorist might think you're going slow enough, or you're going to stop, and decide to cut you off.

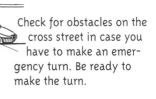

Check for obstacles on the cross street in case you have to make an emergency turn. Be ready to make the turn.

3 If the car suddenly turns, make the emergency turn (see page 147) that puts you alongside the car, avoiding any obstacles.

Approaching an intersection behind a vehicle, no red light.

The motorist slows down, or doesn't speed up to fill the space next to you.

The motorist will let you merge into the next lane.

Merge.

Vehicle slows down or moves slightly to the right.

The car's about to turn.

Slow down, get directly behind, or pass on the other side.

You signal a lane change to a motorist behind you in the next lane.

The motorist speeds up, or continues going fast, to fill the space next to you.

The motorist won't let you in.

Don't merge in front of that car. Signal to one of the next motorists.

BODY LANGUAGE

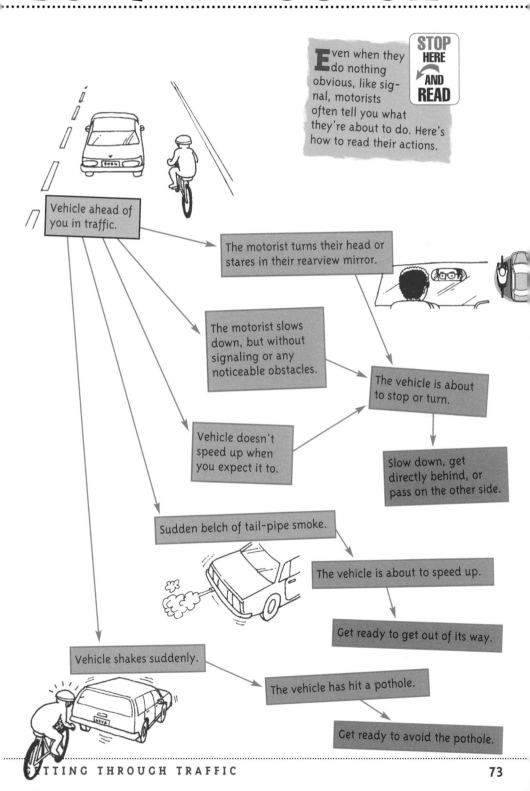

Even when they do nothing obvious, like signal, motorists often tell you what they're about to do. Here's how to read their actions.

STOP HERE AND READ

Vehicle ahead of you in traffic.

The motorist turns their head or stares in their rearview mirror.

The motorist slows down, but without signaling or any noticeable obstacles.

Vehicle doesn't speed up when you expect it to.

The vehicle is about to stop or turn.

Slow down, get directly behind, or pass on the other side.

Sudden belch of tail-pipe smoke.

The vehicle is about to speed up.

Get ready to get out of its way.

Vehicle shakes suddenly.

The vehicle has hit a pothole.

Get ready to avoid the pothole.

Motorists behind you in your lane. You move slightly to the right to let them pass.

The motorist doesn't pass.

The motorist is afraid to pass, about to turn right, or is obeying your area's three-foot pass law.

Wave them through. If they won't go, keep moving—but watch for them to pass.

Smart Idea
Some places have a law forcing motor vehicles to pass bicycles no closer than three feet. Know whether your area has this law.

Car ahead stopped in traffic.

The front wheels are turned.

The car is about to turn or change lanes.

Slow down or pass on the other side.

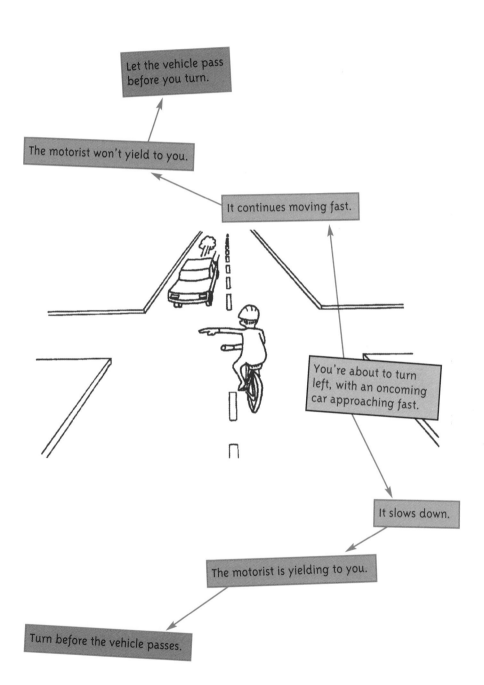

WHEN & HOW

	voice	finger whistle	whistle
noise maker			
cost	none	none	low
likely rip-off	none	none	low
advantages	➤ always available ➤ can use it fast ➤ wide range of tones	➤ always available ➤ louder than voice ➤ can use it fast	➤ can wear it around your neck ➤ others mistake you for police
disadvantages	➤ can't be heard over loud traffic ➤ might not be heard by motorists with closed windows ➤ freaks out pedestrians	➤ must be learned ➤ not everyone can learn it ➤ often requires taking one hand off of handlebars	➤ often requires taking one hand off of handlebars ➤ can hold it between your lips, but gets messy

Kool-Stop "China Bell"

URBAN BIKERS' TRICKS & TIPS

TO MAKE NOISE

"ping" bell

"dong" bell

"ping" bell	"dong" bell
low	low
low	medium
➤ amuses other cyclists	➤ loud at low price
➤ can't be heard in traffic ➤ breaks easily	➤ might not be heard by motorists with closed windows

Recommended Product
Storm whistle
Loud but inexpensive. Have your bike dealer order from All-Weather Safety Whistle, listed under "Bells, Whistles, & Gadgets" in Appendix B. (For more on Mr. Bike's Recommended Products, go to www.mrbike.com/products.)

STOP HERE AND READ

Bikes are slower, quieter, and less visible than most other vehicles. Here's how to make noise that tells people to stay out of your way—especially when you're riding fast.

WHEN IT'S IMPORTANT TO MAKE NOISE

Emerging from between two buildings or large vehicles

Coming to pedestrians in a crosswalk

Riding where a motorist can't see you, and he's about to cut you off

	ball horn	air horn	electronic gizmo
noise maker			
cost	low	medium/high	medium/high
likely rip-off	medium	medium	high
advantages	➤ loud at low price ➤ amuses other cyclists	➤ loud ➤ refill some types using air pump	➤ makes a variety of noises ➤ amuses other cyclists
disadvantages	➤ often requires taking one hand off of handlebars ➤ ball wears out with frequent use	➤ whenever you leave your bike, you must remove it ➤ to avoid theft, must detach easily ➤ you're not sure when it's out of air and won't work	➤ requires batteries ➤ might break in extreme weather ➤ to avoid theft, must detach easily

I can make a noise like a police siren with my mouth. It gets just about anyone out of my way.

Derick Stevens
bicycles in New York City

APPROACHING PEDESTRIANS FROM BEHIND

Consider using a bell if you often encounter peds from behind.

RING RING

Many peds will freak out when you shout at them from behind, causing them to jump in front of you.

ON YOUR LEFT!

LANES & TURNS

When to ride left, when to ride right

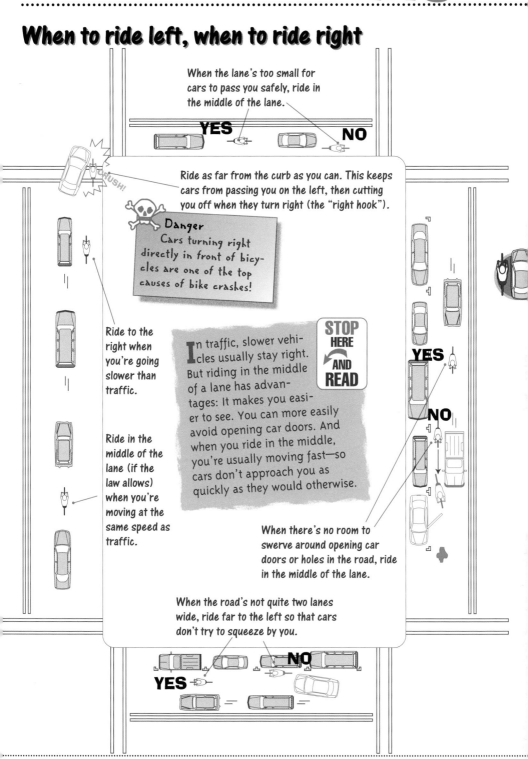

When the lane's too small for cars to pass you safely, ride in the middle of the lane.

YES

NO

Ride as far from the curb as you can. This keeps cars from passing you on the left, then cutting you off when they turn right (the "right hook").

Danger
Cars turning right directly in front of bicycles are one of the top causes of bike crashes!

Ride to the right when you're going slower than traffic.

Ride in the middle of the lane (if the law allows) when you're moving at the same speed as traffic.

STOP HERE AND READ

In traffic, slower vehicles usually stay right. But riding in the middle of a lane has advantages: It makes you easier to see. You can more easily avoid opening car doors. And when you ride in the middle, you're usually moving fast—so cars don't approach you as quickly as they would otherwise.

YES

NO

When there's no room to swerve around opening car doors or holes in the road, ride in the middle of the lane.

When the road's not quite two lanes wide, ride far to the left so that cars don't try to squeeze by you.

YES

NO

Passing on a narrow street

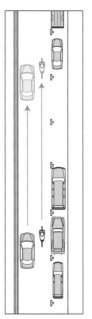

SAFE
Ride in a straight line.

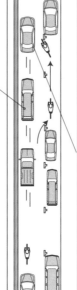

SMART
If you've blocked a bunch of cars on a narrow road, look for a safe place to move right and let them pass.

Before moving left, check traffic behind you. If traffic blocks you, wait for it to clear.

YES

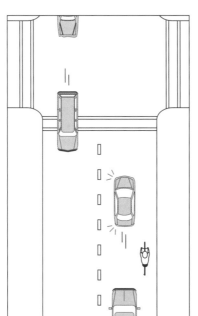

1 While you're riding on the right, the car ahead signals a left turn.

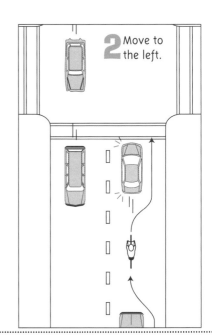

2 Move to the left.

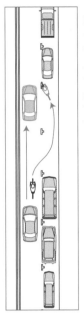

Don't weave in and out of parked cars, because motorists won't see you when you reenter the traffic lane.

NO

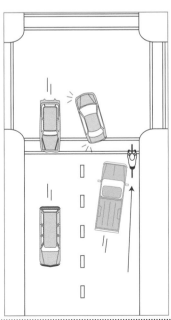

Don't move to where you'll get squeezed by cars passing the turning car.

1 Look back.

2 Move toward the car's left rear end.

3 Snake around the car to avoid other vehicles that might pass.

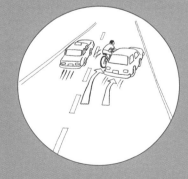

Stopping at Red Lights

CARS STOPPED IN BOTH LANES

SMART

If the right-lane car is waiting to turn right, stop on the left side of the right lane. Move to where motorists on both sides can see you.

SAFE

Stop in the middle of the right lane.

WITH RIGHT ON RED ALLOWED

If there's room for right-turning cars, stop on the left side of the right lane so they can get past you. If a car's stopped in the left lane, stop where motorists on both sides can see you.

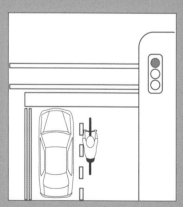

Where to go in a multi-lane intersection

1 When approaching the inter-section, figure out the lane sets: which set of lanes goes straight, which set goes left, and which set goes right.

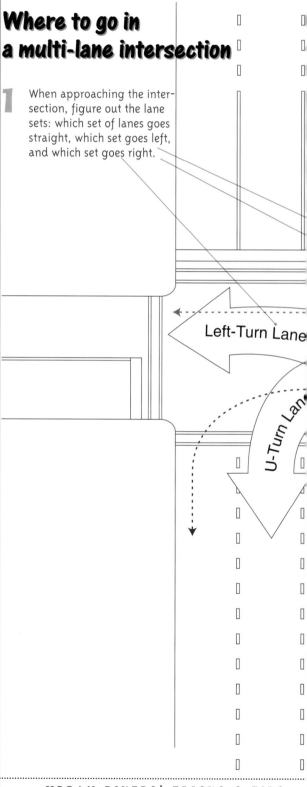

Left-Turn Lane

U-Turn Lane

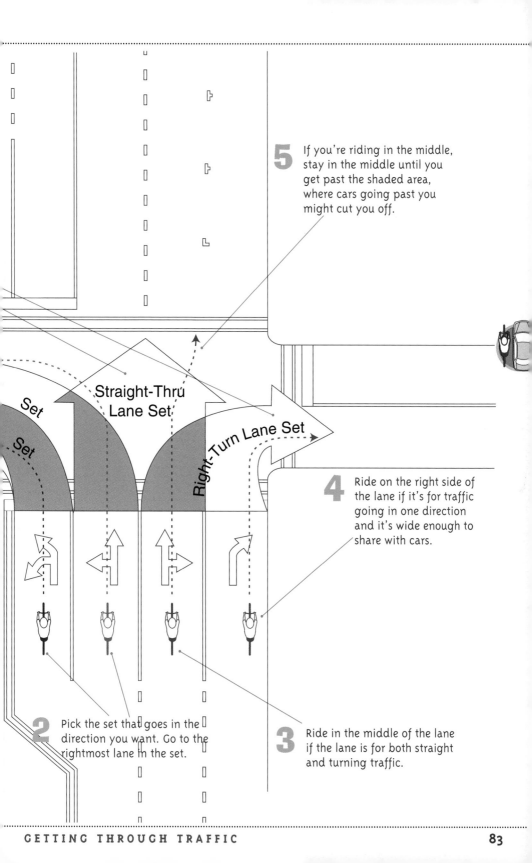

5 If you're riding in the middle, stay in the middle until you get past the shaded area, where cars going past you might cut you off.

Straight-Thru Lane Set

Set

Set

Right-Turn Lane Set

4 Ride on the right side of the lane if it's for traffic going in one direction and it's wide enough to share with cars.

2 Pick the set that goes in the direction you want. Go to the rightmost lane in the set.

3 Ride in the middle of the lane if the lane is for both straight and turning traffic.

The basic left turn

1 Look behind you for a gap in traffic. When traffic allows, signal left and change lanes.

If you can't find a gap, get a driver to let you in by making eye contact and pointing.

2 When you're turning left on a multi-lane street where traffic isn't much faster than you, merge left one lane at a time.

Where traffic moves much faster, wait for a gap in traffic and move across all the lanes at once.

3 Get into the left-turn lane. More than one turn lane? Use the one farthest to the right—unless you're making another left turn immediately.

5 When there's a gap in oncoming traffic, finish the turn. Move into the right lane—unless another vehicle is there, or you're making another left turn right away.

4 **SAFE**
Get directly behind the last car waiting to turn left.

SLY
Get behind the right rear bumper of the first car in line, out of the way of cars in the next lane.

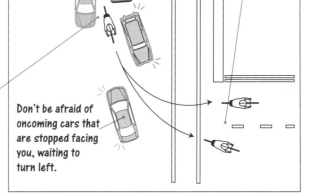

Don't be afraid of oncoming cars that are stopped facing you, waiting to turn left.

The box left turn

1 Stay in the right lane and ride across the intersection on the left side of the crosswalk.

Use the box left turn if you can't merge left before you reach the intersection, or the left-turn lane is jammed.

STOP HERE AND READ

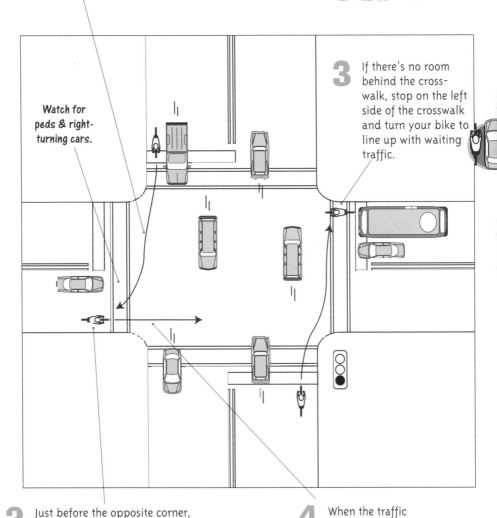

Watch for peds & right-turning cars.

3 If there's no room behind the crosswalk, stop on the left side of the crosswalk and turn your bike to line up with waiting traffic.

2 Just before the opposite corner, check whether there's room for you in the traffic lane to the right of the crosswalk. If so, go there and turn your bike to line up with waiting traffic.

4 When the traffic light changes, move with traffic.

The impatient left turn

Sly Bikers Only!

SITUATION:

➢ Red light.

➢ Before you get through the left-turn lane, you might have to wait for two green lights.

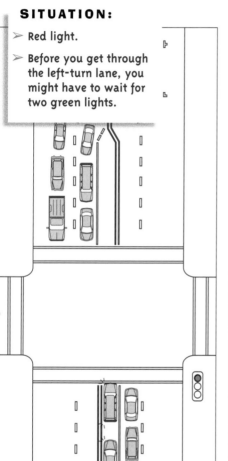

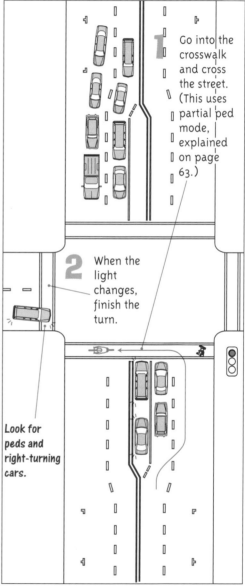

1 Go into the crosswalk and cross the street. (This uses partial ped mode, explained on page 63.)

2 When the light changes, finish the turn.

Look for peds and right-turning cars.

The shortcut left turn

Sly Bikers Only!

SITUATION:

➤ Green light.

➤ Before you get thru the left-turn lane, the light might turn red.

➤ Oncoming traffic hasn't reached the intersection.

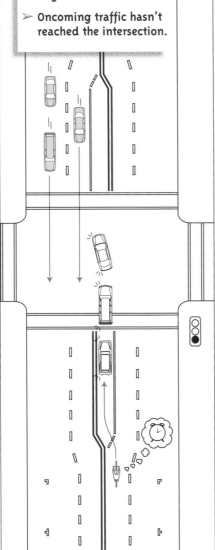

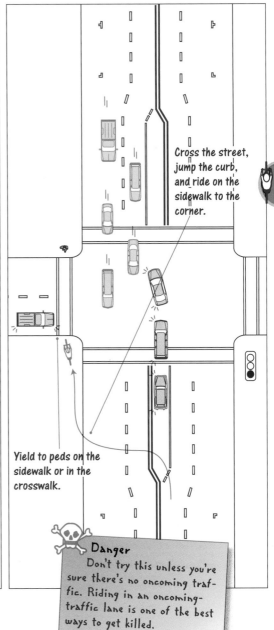

Cross the street, jump the curb, and ride on the sidewalk to the corner.

Yield to peds on the sidewalk or in the crosswalk.

Danger

Don't try this unless you're sure there's no oncoming traffic. Riding in an oncoming-traffic lane is one of the best ways to get killed.

Special left-turn cases

Some places use right-hand exits for left turns. Use these tips to save time.

STOP HERE AND READ

If the light for straight-through traffic is green

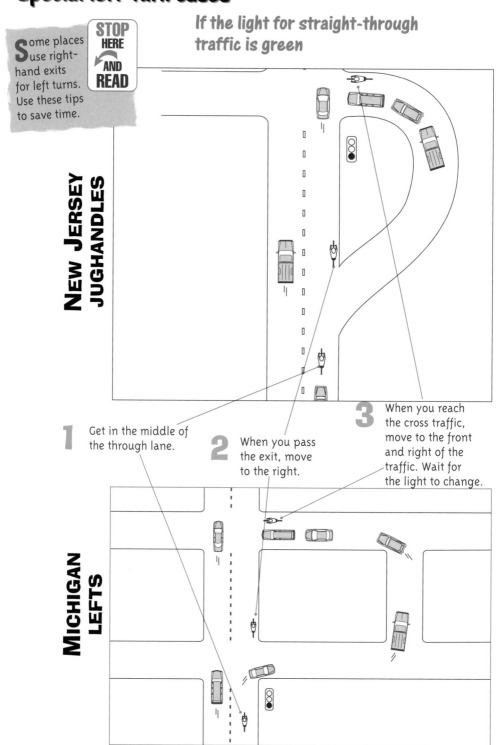

NEW JERSEY JUGHANDLES

MICHIGAN LEFTS

1 Get in the middle of the through lane.

2 When you pass the exit, move to the right.

3 When you reach the cross traffic, move to the front and right of the traffic. Wait for the light to change.

If the light for straight-through traffic is about to turn red

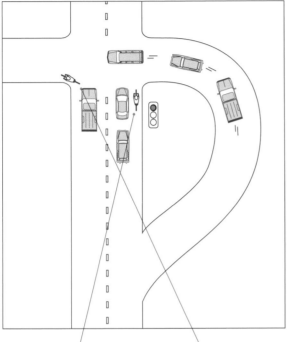

1 Ride straight to the cross traffic.

2 As the light changes, turn left and merge with the cross traffic.

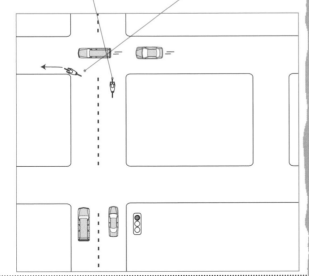

NO LEFT-TURN LANE

If there's no turn lane, ride at least three feet from the center stripe so a left-turning car behind you can't pass you on the right.

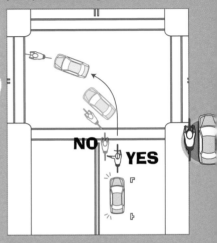

NO **YES**

LEFT TURN ON RED

When turning left from a one-way street to another one-way, don't forget that many cities allow left turns on red. (After the turn, stay left if you're going left again.)

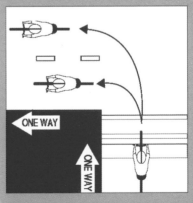

ONE WAY

ONE WAY

Obstacles in bike lanes

Problem:
Motorists often use bike lanes to double park. Also, some bike lanes are placed in the door zone.

Solution: Keep an eye on traffic in the lane next to you, either by turning your head or with a mirror, in case you have to swerve out of the bike lane.

Sly Bikers Only! Try to ride nearly as fast as the traffic in the adjacent lane. When obstacles arise, look back, signal if you can, and ride in the adjacent lane as far as you have to.

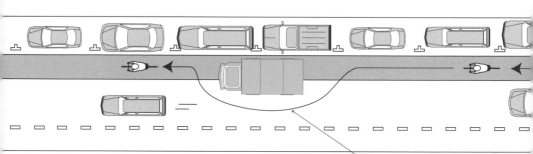

If it seems easiest, stay in the adjacent lane.

Bike lanes at intersections

Problem:
When preparing to turn, motorists might go anywhere: in the bike lane, to the left of the lane, or to the right of the lane.

Solution: As you approach an intersection, take a lane position that makes you most visible (see page 82). But be ready to avoid a motorist who might cut you off.

In drive-through restaurants or banks, stay in the middle of the lane so cars don't pass you.

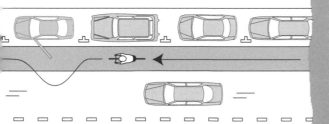

Crossing an intersection

SAFE

When you cross an intersection don't veer to the left or right. Ride in a straight line that tells motorists exactly where you plan to go.

Veering right makes it harder for cross traffic to see you.

SMART

If you've blocked a bunch of cars on a narrow road:

When you cross an intersection move over to let them pass.

Before you reenter the traffic lane, look back for more traffic.

Setting up for a right turn

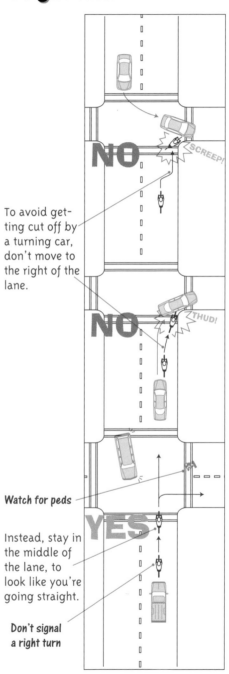

To avoid getting cut off by a turning car, don't move to the right of the lane.

Watch for peds

Instead, stay in the middle of the lane, to look like you're going straight.

Don't signal a right turn

Bus Traffic

Turning right behind a stopped bus

SITUATION:

You want to turn right at a corner where a bus has stopped.

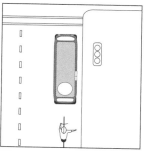

If your light is red, don't turn in front of the bus unless you know it won't change to green during your turn (see page 100).

N O

Many bus drivers will start moving early!

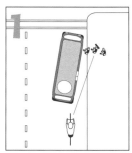

Don't turn in front of the bus unless you see passengers will still be boarding while you turn.

Buses are funny vehicles. They stop, spit out passengers, go, stop, spit out some more . . . easy to predict, right? Not for some cyclists: They get cut off by buses, or nearly get hit when they try to pass buses. But this doesn't have to happen to you. Learn the tricks on these pages and you can handle buses, no matter what they do.

PASSING A STOPPED TROLLEY

You're about to come alongside a trolley or light-rail train that has just stopped.

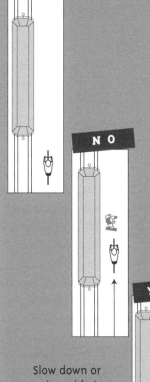

N O

Y E S

Slow down or swing wide to avoid passengers.

Bus follows you, but doesn't pass

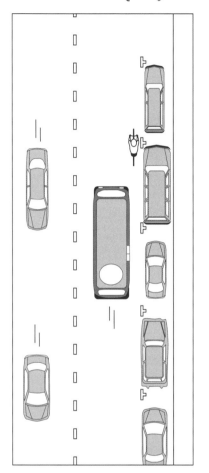

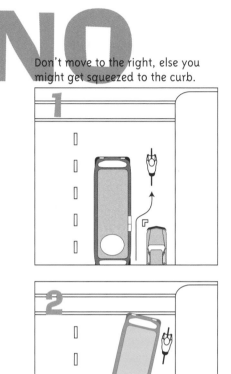

NO

Don't move to the right, else you might get squeezed to the curb.

Bus starts to pass just before a bus stop

Prepare for the bus to cut you off:
- ➤ Slow down and check traffic behind you.
- ➤ Get ready to move left and pass the bus, or to stop suddenly.

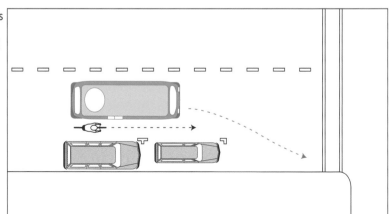

YES

Keep your speed up and ride in a straight line.

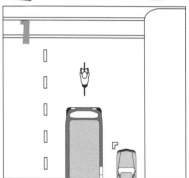

1

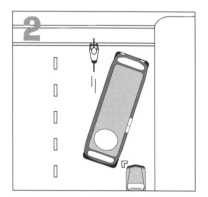

2

1 If keeping up your speed makes you feel like you're cutting the bus off,

2 Slow down and check traffic behind you.

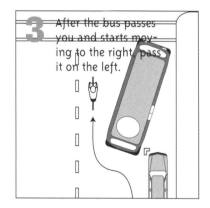

3 After the bus passes you and starts moving to the right, pass it on the left.

Smart Idea
If you continually get harassed by a particular bus driver, note the bus number and time. Each time you get harassed, report it to the bus agency. Also report drivers who you think drive very well around cyclists.

Passing a bus stopped at a bus stop

Pass left

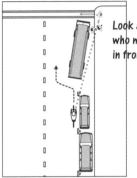

Pass right

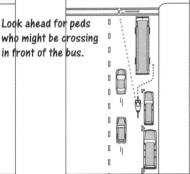

Look ahead for peds who might be crossing in front of the bus.

SITUATION:

You approach a bus stopped at a bus stop.

Pass left if: Passengers will still be getting on by the time you reach the bus.

Pass right if:
➢ There's room.
➢ You don't want to slow down.
➢ You can see that all passengers have finished getting on or off.

Wait

YES

Wait if there's no room.

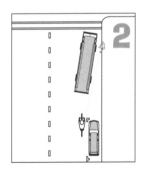

Wait if by the time you reach the bus, passengers will finish getting on or off.

NO

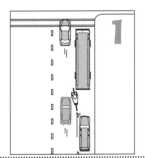

NO

With a single lane in each direction, don't pass if you can't escape from surprise traffic.

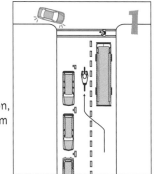

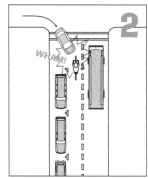

YES

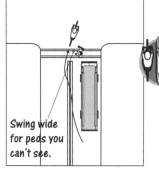

Swing wide for peds you can't see.

1 Move to the left of the lane and look into the oncoming lane.

2 Pass left if there's room.

Leapfrogging buses

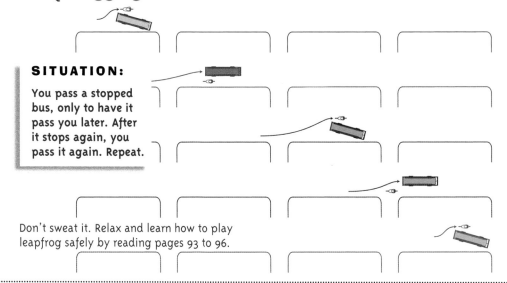

SITUATION:

You pass a stopped bus, only to have it pass you later. After it stops again, you pass it again. Repeat.

Don't sweat it. Relax and learn how to play leapfrog safely by reading pages 93 to 96.

Ramps

Two ways to pass entrance ramps

Move straight

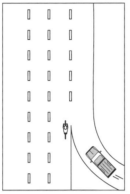

So that motorists can better judge your speed, keep it constant.

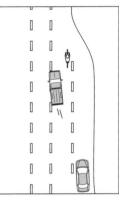

1 Look over your right shoulder to see what's coming.

2 If you see a lot of vehicles, stay straight so the vehicles in front pass you on the right.

3 As you move farther, the rest of the vehicles will pass behind you and on your left.

Cut right

1 Look over your right shoulder to see what's coming.

2 If you see a break in the ramp traffic, move right.

3 Vehicles will pass you on your left.

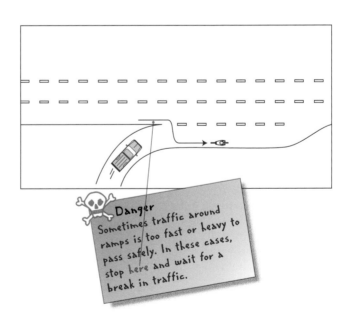

☠ Danger
Sometimes traffic around ramps is too fast or heavy to pass safely. In these cases, stop here and wait for a break in traffic.

Two ways to pass exit ramps

Stay in the through lane

1 Look over your left shoulder to see what's coming.

2 If traffic looks light or slow-moving, signal left and move to the middle of the through lane.

3 Traffic will pass you on the right.

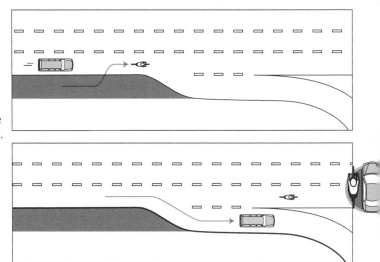

Move right, cut left

1 Look over your left shoulder to see what's coming.

2 If you see a lot of vehicles, move to the right side or shoulder of the exit lane. Vehicles will pass you on your left.

3 When you reach the exit ramp, look back. If there's no break in traffic, stop and wait. Then cut left across the exit ramp.

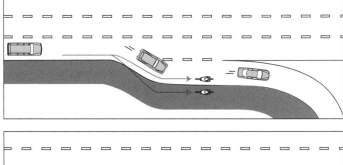

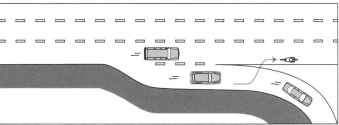

If motorists don't seem to know what you'll do, wave them on. Then cross the ramp behind them.

TIMING

Learning how to use the DON'T WALK signal

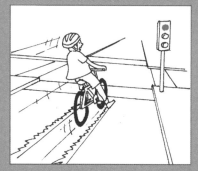

THE PROBLEM:

Just when you speed up to get through an intersection, the light changes —so you have to stop.

1 WATCH

Stop at red lights (if you don't already) and watch the DON'T WALK signal facing traffic in the cross street. Wait for it to change from WALK to DON'T WALK.

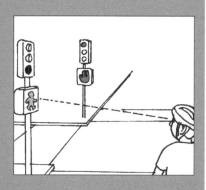

THE SOLUTION:

Learn to guess when a green light will change by watching the DON'T WALK signal.

TRAFFIC LIGHTS

2 COUNT

Count the seconds the DON'T WALK signal stays on before the traffic light turns red. If the signal flashes, count the number of flashes before the signal turns green.

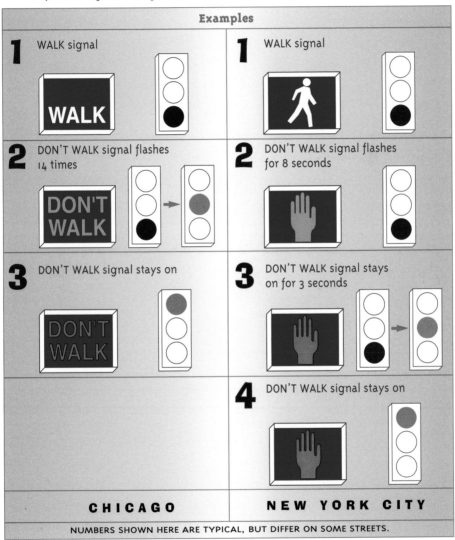

Examples

1 WALK signal

1 WALK signal

2 DON'T WALK signal flashes 14 times

2 DON'T WALK signal flashes for 8 seconds

3 DON'T WALK signal stays on

3 DON'T WALK signal stays on for 3 seconds

4 DON'T WALK signal stays on

CHICAGO

NEW YORK CITY

NUMBERS SHOWN HERE ARE TYPICAL, BUT DIFFER ON SOME STREETS.

3 REMEMBER

You'll find that many intersections use the same DON'T WALK signal timing. Remember the timing for the intersections you use often.

Using traffic-light timing

1 LOOK

The first thing you should do when you approach an intersection is look for the DON'T WALK signal facing your way.

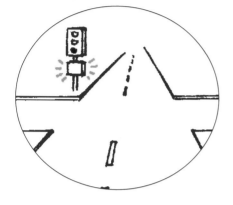

2 COUNT

When the signal changes from a steady WALK signal, start counting, according to the timing you've already figured.

3 DECIDE

Decide whether you can get through the intersection before your light changes from green. If not, slow down.

Close enough to make the green

Too far away to make the green

Pedestrian-controlled signals

At intersections with pedestrian-controlled signals, watch for a ped pressing a button to make the traffic light turn green. The DON'T WALK signal might flash longer than usual.

GOING THROUGH YELLOW LIGHTS

YES

If the traffic light turns yellow just before you reach the intersection, keep your speed up or stop.

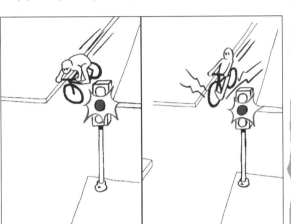

NO

Don't slow down while going through the intersection. You make yourself a target.

Sly Bikers Only! If an oncoming car's waiting to turn left, maintain your speed—but get ready to go around the car, stop, or make an emergency turn (see page 147).

If the light will turn red while you're crossing the intersection, try to "shadow" (ride alongside) a car that's also crossing the intersection. Shadowing lets you keep your speed up.

RED LIGHTS

SITUATION:

Cross traffic has just gotten the green. Motorists take a second or two to start moving.

Cyclists who take advantage of motorists' hesitation will blast through the intersection.

As you go through the intersection, swing out to your left to avoid motorists who begin to move, and to make yourself more visible to them.

Also use this technique when motorists at stop signs might not see you.

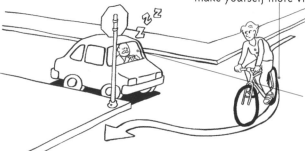

WHAT TO WATCH OUT FOR

Intersections with a 4-way red light that allows diagonal pedestrian crossing.

Where police might stop you for running a red light, go into ped mode: use the crosswalk.

Intersections that have red light cameras. (To learn what U.S. towns use them go to www.iihs.org/laws/auto_enforce_cities.aspx.)

Before you run lights, make sure your bike's in good shape. When you run lights, you often must move or stop suddenly— and a bike with bad brakes or a bad drive train (chain, gears, and hubs) will choke.

T^HE 3-STREET

HOW LIGHTS CHANGE AT 3-STREET INTERSECTIONS

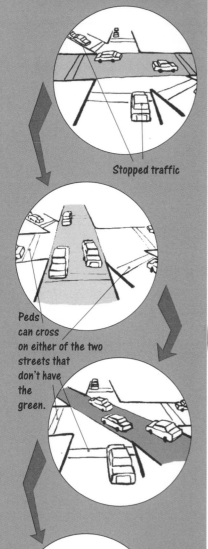

Stopped traffic

Peds can cross on either of the two streets that don't have the green.

1 After the light on your street turns red, go to the cross-walk and turn left (in ped mode).

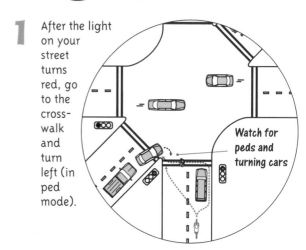

Watch for peds and turning cars

2 Cross the next street and wait on the corner.

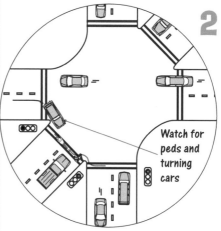

Watch for peds and turning cars

3 Wait here or here so turn-ing cars don't hit you.

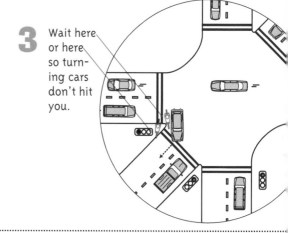

RUN-AROUND

4 When the light changes, cross the third street. Watch for peds & turning cars.

When the light turns red at the intersection of three streets, you have to wait twice as long for the green. If you don't want to wait, you can use the 3-street runaround to cut your wait time in half. You do it by going into ped mode, and using the crosswalk on the cross street where traffic is stopped.

STOP HERE AND READ

Sly Bikers Only! At least a block ahead, keep track of when your light changes.

5 Go through the crosswalk on your original street, turn left into your lane, and continue your ride.

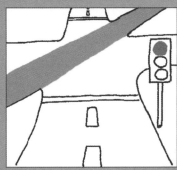

If your light turns red too soon, by the time you reach the intersection it'll be too late to do the 3-street runaround.

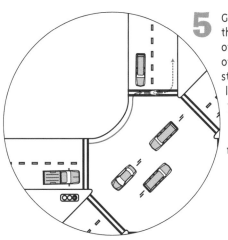

1 Cross your street
2 Cross next street
3 Wait
4 Cross third street
5 Continue

MAKING

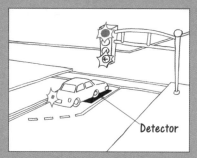

> Activate a left-turn signal

Normally stays green

Detector

> On a busy street, change a green light to red so traffic on a quiet cross street can go
> Make a green light stay green longer

Recommended Product
Green Light Trigger
A magnet that straps to the bottom of your bike's pedal or crank to trigger detectors. Order from Kauffman Marketing, listed under "Bells, Whistles, & Gadgets" in Appendix B. (For more on Mr. Bike's Recommended Products, go to www.mrbike.com/products.)

Some traffic lights change the same way all the time—for example, every 30 seconds. But other ones will stay green longer—or turn green sooner—when there's more traffic. How? They use a piece of wire, called a **detector,** buried under the street. The detector can tell when a vehicle is stopped on the street on top of the detector. Then it can make a traffic light stay on until the vehicle has passed.

STOP HERE AND READ

What to look for

Square cut in the pavement

Round cut in the pavement

TRAFFIC LIGHTS TURN GREEN

Where to stop

Try both ways (at different times) to see which works better.

Some detectors work best when you stop over the middle. If you see pavement cuts in the middle, stop over the cuts.

Others detectors work best when you stop on the edge.

Smart Idea
Don't worry about people pressing pedestrian buttons. They usually have no effect when you activate a detector.

How they work

Detectors sense the metal in a vehicle.

Bikes don't have enough metal to trip the detectors in many places. The only way to tell whether your bike will activate a detector: Try it!

Detectors marked for bikes

WHAT DETECTORS DO

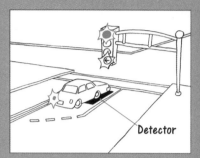

➤ Activate a left-turn signal

Normally stays green

Detector

➤ On a busy street, change a green light to red so traffic on a quiet cross street can go
➤ Make a green light stay green longer

💡 Smart Idea
If your bike never makes the detector work, the detector might need repair or adjustment. Call your local department of transportation to report it. (Traffic engineers call the detectors "detector loops.")

If a traffic lane just before an intersection is marked with a bicycle symbol, stop your bike over it.

If it doesn't work:
The detectors work by sensing the metal in your bike. If you stop over the symbol and it doesn't affect the traffic light, get off of your bike and lay it down on top of the symbol. This gives the detector more metal to detect. (Also see the "Recommended Product" on p. 108.)

Detector left vs. shortcut left

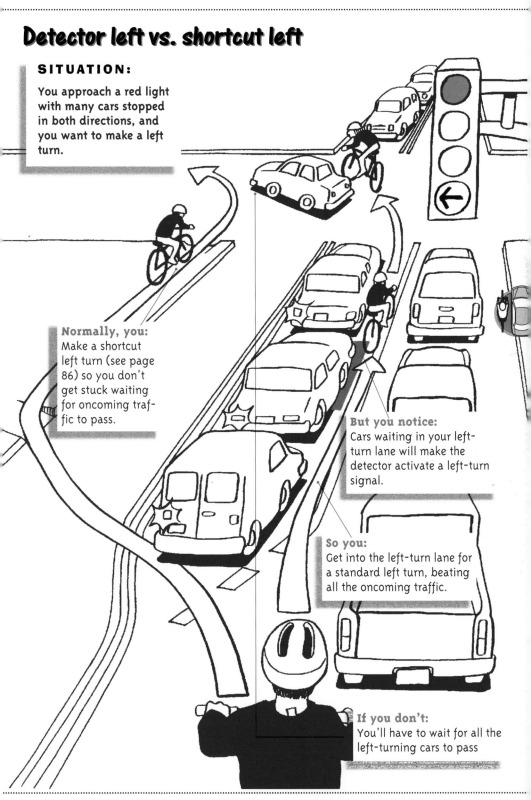

SITUATION:

You approach a red light with many cars stopped in both directions, and you want to make a left turn.

Normally, you:
Make a shortcut left turn (see page 86) so you don't get stuck waiting for oncoming traffic to pass.

But you notice:
Cars waiting in your left-turn lane will make the detector activate a left-turn signal.

So you:
Get into the left-turn lane for a standard left turn, beating all the oncoming traffic.

If you don't:
You'll have to wait for all the left-turning cars to pass

TIMING

RIDING SINGLE FILE

Some traffic lights will stay green as long as vehicles pass over the detectors. When you ride through such intersections with other bicyclists, you should ride single file so the light stays green for everyone.

Where traffic lights aren't timed for bikes, a detector might keep the light green long enough for a car to get through.

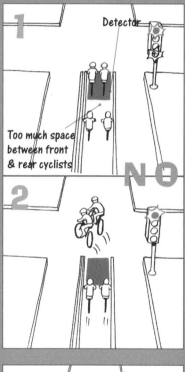

Detector

Too much space between front & rear cyclists

NO

YES

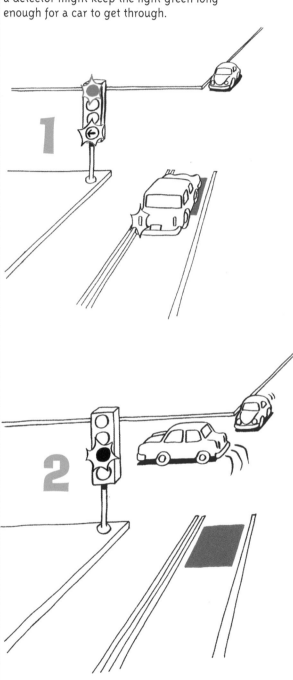

PAVEMENT DETECTORS

Where traffic lights aren't timed for bikes, a detector might not keep the light green long enough for a bicycle to get through the intersection.

Watch out for traffic that won't wait for you

THE DOOR ZONE:

The three or four feet next to parked cars in which you could get hit by an opening door.

Why ride in the door zone?

You're going faster than traff and the only room to pass lies within the door zone.

A delivery vehicle or taxi stops in traffic, so you pass on the right.

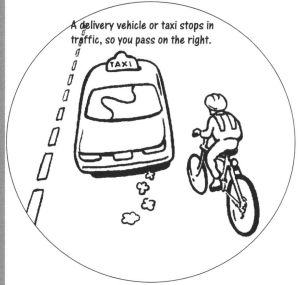

THE DOOR ZONE

How to avoid getting doored

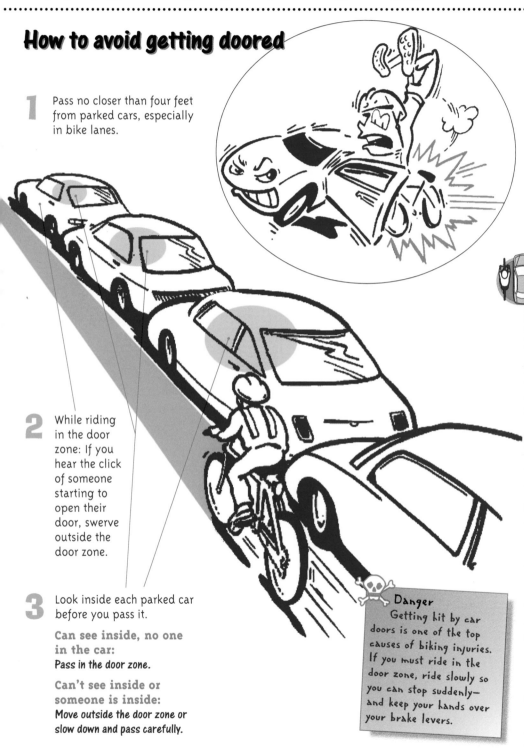

1 Pass no closer than four feet from parked cars, especially in bike lanes.

2 While riding in the door zone: If you hear the click of someone starting to open their door, swerve outside the door zone.

3 Look inside each parked car before you pass it.

Can see inside, no one in the car:
Pass in the door zone.

Can't see inside or someone is inside:
Move outside the door zone or slow down and pass carefully.

Danger
Getting hit by car doors is one of the top causes of biking injuries. If you must ride in the door zone, ride slowly so you can stop suddenly— and keep your hands over your brake levers.

Watching behind you in the door zone

In the door zone, keep track of what's behind you: If you have to swerve suddenly, you could get hit by traffic. Also, look for stretches where you can ride out of the door zone.

LISTEN FOR TRAFFIC COMING

You know that this truck doesn't give you room to swerve out of the door zone.

So the next time you hear it behind you, you move out of the zone before the truck can pass.

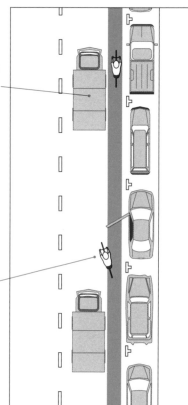

LOOK BEHIND YOU A LOT

Look over your shoulder frequently

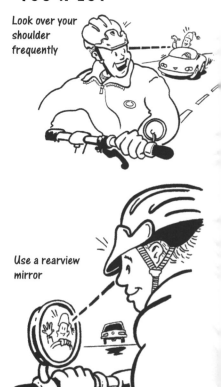

Use a rearview mirror

TRAFFIC JAMS

Squeezing between stopped cars

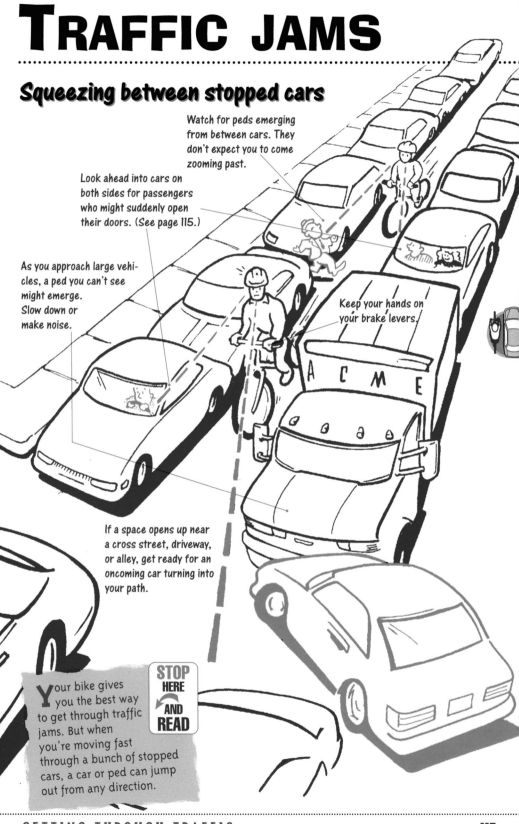

Watch for peds emerging from between cars. They don't expect you to come zooming past.

Look ahead into cars on both sides for passengers who might suddenly open their doors. (See page 115.)

As you approach large vehicles, a ped you can't see might emerge. Slow down or make noise.

Keep your hands on your brake levers.

If a space opens up near a cross street, driveway, or alley, get ready for an oncoming car turning into your path.

STOP HERE AND READ

Your bike gives you the best way to get through traffic jams. But when you're moving fast through a bunch of stopped cars, a car or ped can jump out from any direction.

Riding the center line

If traffic in your direction is completely jammed, and you've no room in the door zone, ride on the center line or on the lane stripe between lanes.

Watch for oncoming vehicles that leave you no space to ride.

If you can't avoid oncoming traffic, move over and stop.

If there's no oncoming traffic, watch the front wheels of cars ahead.

HEY!

Turning wheels might indicate an impatient motorist about to pull out in front of you.

If you time it right, you can ride into the space (without slowing down) before the car behind closes the space.

GETTING INTO A LANE FROM THE CENTER LINE

When traffic starts to move, watch the spaces between the front cars open up.

Eventually you'll get next to a space that has opened up.

RIDING UNDER

STOP
HERE
↖
AND
READ

Streets underneath elevated rail tracks can be the fastest to ride on. Why? There's often room to ride between the track posts and the door zone. The track posts keep cars from moving to the right, so cars stay out of your way.

When cars jam up, pass on the other side of the posts, or on the motorists' left.

Danger
Riding against traffic is always dangerous. Elevated tracks make it worse, because you and motorists can't see each other until the last second.

Watch for motorists turning right at intersections. They often turn from the outside lane, where track posts block their view of you.

ELEVATED
RAIL TRACKS

Danger
If you ride outside the posts even
if there's not enough room
to avoid the door zone, watch
carefully for passengers who might
open doors. The track posts don't
give you room to swerve.

As each post becomes visible, look to the outside for peds. A ped who looks only for cars might walk in front of you.

Ride on the outside of the posts when you have enough room to avoid the door zone. Otherwise ride on the inside of the posts.

SHORT ATTENTION

Rating (5 = most danger)	Action	
	Ride against traffic on street	
	Ride on a sidewalk against traffic	
	Ride on a sidewalk in the direction of traffic	
	Fail to yield	
	Ride at night without lights	
	Run a stop sign or red light	
	Turn left from wrong position	
	Swerve unexpectedly	
	Ride too close to a parked vehicle	
	Proceed straight from a right-turn lane	
	Pass vehicles on right near intersection	

Possible result
Get hit by a vehicle going straight, turning, or leaving a parking space, from any direction
Get hit by a vehicle turning into or emerging from a cross street, alley, or driveway
Hit or get hit by a pedestrian, or hit an object while avoiding a pedestrian
Get hit by a vehicle turning into or emerging from a cross street, alley, or driveway
Hit or get hit by a vehicle going straight, left, or right
Get hit by a vehicle going straight, turning, or leaving a parking space, from any direction
Get hit by a pedestrian
Hit or get hit by a vehicle turning into or traveling down a cross street
Get hit by a vehicle traveling straight, from behind or in front of you
Vehicle rear-ends or sideswipes you
Get hit by an opening vehicle door
Get hit by a vehicle turning right
Get hit by a vehicle turning right

STOP HERE AND READ

Most cyclists involved in crashes get hit from ahead, not behind. And often, cyclists get hit from behind because they swerve into the motorist's path—so you're pretty safe if you ride in a straight line. But what moves *do* put you most at risk? Different studies don't agree exactly. So we've condensed a bunch of the studies into this table.

Sly Bikers Only! In heavy traffic, if you act like a wimp and hesitate a lot, motorists will become impatient, and even run you off the road—accidentally or not. Riding less like a wimp makes you safer in traffic, according to something called Komanoff's Rule.

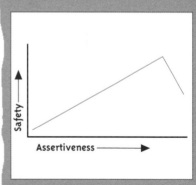

Graph of Komanoff's Rule

Komanoff's Rule says the more assertively you ride, the safer you become. In other words, when you act like the vehicles around you, motorists see you as one of them—so neither of you will surprise the other.

But if you get **too** assertive, you become reckless. Then nobody can predict what you'll do next—meaning there's a better chance you'll get clobbered.

TROUBLE SITUATIONS

Out on the street, **trouble's waiting for you**. Trouble might look like man's best friend, the dog. It might look like a car with a bad muffler. Or some dude staring at you from the curb. Or just a pothole.

Page 145

Page 132

Maybe you've never met up with trouble on your bike. But one day, you might: You'll get a scrape, get mugged, or even crash. **What can you do? This chapter tells you.**

Page 126

The first time trouble kicks your butt, you won't have time to think. You might freak out—maybe freak out so much, **you might not want to get back on your bike**. This chapter tells you how to deal with that.

Page 143

When trouble hits, maybe you'll get mad. **You might want to hit back.** This chapter tells you about that too.

Page 136

You might never need this chapter. But it has some **tips that can save you time, money, or even injury** if you run into trouble. Have a look.

Page 148

WHEN A MOTORIST

At the crash site

Get treated
Don't stop paramedics from examining you or taking you to the hospital.
Why?
➤ After a crash, you get very excited. You might not notice that you've bruised, broken, or torn some part of your body—until later.
➤ Sometimes, the motorist's auto insurance will cover your medical costs—so even if you have no medical coverage, you can still afford a hospital visit. To learn more, contact your local bike advocacy group (see Appendix A).

Hit and Run

➤ If a motorist hits you and doesn't stop, unless you're badly injured, go to the nearest police station and ask to make a report.
➤ If you're injured by a hit-and-run motorist, call police from the hospital and ask to make a report.
➤ Then follow the steps on pages 128 and 129.
➤ Why make a police report? You or police might later identify the motorist. Then you can take action.

Smart Ideas

➤ Sometimes cops don't make police reports for bike crashes. You need one to support your claims. If police aren't making a report, politely explain that you'll need one when you take the motorist to court.
➤ Some cops are on power trips. Address them as "sir" or "ma'am," and if you argue, don't yell. Also, refer to police as "officers," not cops.

Get location info
Write down the nearby street names, nearest street address, time, date, weather conditions, and the direction of travel taken by you and the other involved vehicles.

Call police
Have someone call police. If you're hurt, have them call for an ambulance or paramedics.

HITS YOU

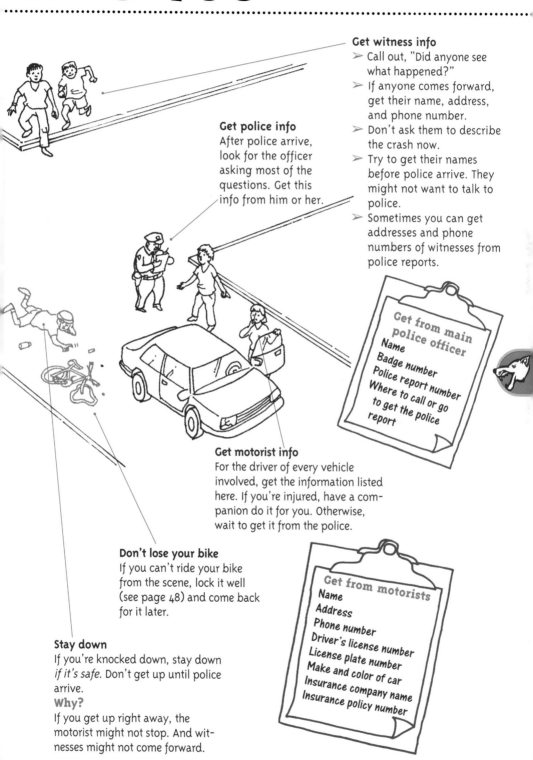

Get witness info
> Call out, "Did anyone see what happened?"
> If anyone comes forward, get their name, address, and phone number.
> Don't ask them to describe the crash now.
> Try to get their names before police arrive. They might not want to talk to police.
> Sometimes you can get addresses and phone numbers of witnesses from police reports.

Get police info
After police arrive, look for the officer asking most of the questions. Get this info from him or her.

Get from main police officer
Name
Badge number
Police report number
Where to call or go to get the police report

Get motorist info
For the driver of every vehicle involved, get the information listed here. If you're injured, have a companion do it for you. Otherwise, wait to get it from the police.

Don't lose your bike
If you can't ride your bike from the scene, lock it well (see page 48) and come back for it later.

Get from motorists
Name
Address
Phone number
Driver's license number
License plate number
Make and color of car
Insurance company name
Insurance policy number

Stay down
If you're knocked down, stay down *if it's safe.* Don't get up until police arrive.
Why?
If you get up right away, the motorist might not stop. And witnesses might not come forward.

At the hospital

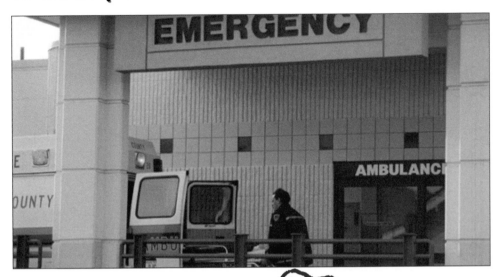

1 **Don't sign anything**
A police officer or other official might ask you to sign an accident report "just as a formality." Don't do it—especially if you're shaken up. You might be admitting blame.

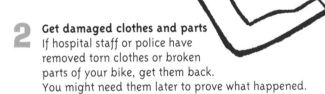

2 **Get damaged clothes and parts**
If hospital staff or police have removed torn clothes or broken parts of your bike, get them back. You might need them later to prove what happened.

After you get home

1 Write stuff down
Write down everything you can remember about the crash.

2 Record damage
➤ Take photos of any clothes or bike equipment that got damaged.
➤ Get a repair estimate for your bike from a bike-repair shop. And if your clothes were damaged, find out the replacement cost.

3 Look for witnesses
The next day, go back to the scene of the crash and look for witnesses. Look for building lobbies, stores, newspaper stands, and taxi-cab waiting areas. Go to these and ask people if they saw the crash. If they did, ask them if they'd like to help you prove your case.

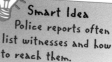

Smart Idea
Police reports often list witnesses and how to reach them.

4 Ask for statements
For each witness:
➤ Call or meet with them. Get them to describe what happened. Use a tape recorder or take written notes. (Don't coach them!)
➤ Type up what each witness said, and show it to them. Correct the parts they have problems with.
➤ Ask them to sign the statement.

Asking for money after a crash

When should you ask the motorist or their insurer for money?

1 You want your medical bills paid.

2 You want someone to pay for your damaged bike.

$

What insurance companies usually pay for

➢ Medical costs

➢ Damaged property (clothes, bicycle, glasses)

➢ Wages you lost due to time off

➢ "Pain & suffering" (two to three times your medical costs)

Lawyers

YOU MIGHT NOT NEED A LAWYER IF:

➢ Police have clearly cited the motorist (and not you) for doing something wrong.

➢ The motorist is insured.

➢ You're willing to negotiate with the insurance company.

➢ Your area has no-fault insurance: The motorist's insurance automatically covers your medical expenses.

YOU MIGHT NEED A LAWYER IF:

The motorist tries to get you to pay for vehicle damages. The motorist might back down if you have a lawyer.

HOW TO FIND A LAWYER

You can find lawyers in your city who handle bicycle cases. They often charge nothing unless they help win your case, and then charge only a part of your settlement. In the U.S., your local bike-advocacy group might know bike-smart lawyers to whom they can refer you. See "Local advocacy groups" in Appendix A.

WHAT A LAWYER SHOULD CHARGE YOU

1 If a lawyer helps you get money ("a settlement") from the motorist or insurer, they should get a percentage of the money. If you receive no money, a lawyer should not charge you.

2 Some lawyers charge extra for certain items, such as deliveries. Make sure they take those charges out of *their* percentage of the settlement so *you* don't pay extra.

3 Some lawyers charge one percentage to negotiate with an insurer, and charge a higher percentage if your case goes to court. Ask about that up front. Ask your lawyer to charge the same in both situations.

4 Before you hire any lawyer, always ask them to put their charges in writing.

Making a demand package

WHAT IT DOES

➤ It's what lawyers send and insurance companies expect—but you can do it yourself.

➤ Goes to insurer or motorist (if not insured).

➤ Proves why they should give you money.

➤ Tells exactly what happened.

➤ Shows what you lost that you want to get paid for.

➤ Send it after you've gotten all your medical bills—especially if treatment takes a long time.

COVER-LETTER EXAMPLE

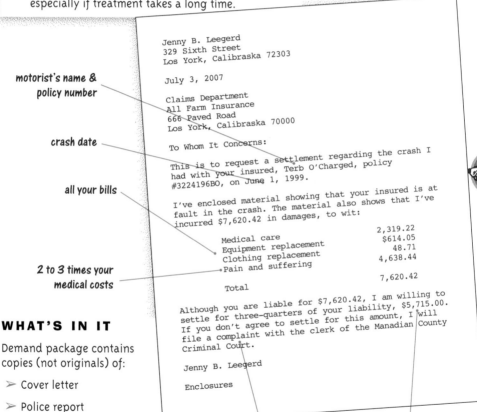

motorist's name & policy number

crash date

all your bills

2 to 3 times your medical costs

Jenny B. Leegerd
329 Sixth Street
Los York, Calibraska 72303

July 3, 2007

Claims Department
All Farm Insurance
666 Paved Road
Los York, Calibraska 70000

To Whom It Concerns:

This is to request a settlement regarding the crash I had with your insured, Terb O'Charged, policy #3224196BO, on June 1, 1999.

I've enclosed material showing that your insured is at fault in the crash. The material also shows that I've incurred $7,620.42 in damages, to wit:

Medical care	2,319.22
Equipment replacement	$614.05
Clothing replacement	48.71
Pain and suffering	4,638.44
Total	7,620.42

Although you are liable for $7,620.42, I am willing to settle for three-quarters of your liability, $5,715.00. If you don't agree to settle for this amount, I will file a complaint with the clerk of the Manadian County Criminal Court.

Jenny B. Leegerd

Enclosures

if you don't get it, you'll sue

how much you'll settle for

WHAT'S IN IT

Demand package contains copies (not originals) of:

➤ Cover letter

➤ Police report

➤ Written, signed statements of one or more witnesses

➤ Repair or replacement bills (or estimates) for your bike and clothes

➤ Photographs of your damaged bike and clothes

How to PREVENT ATTACKS

Know your route
If you don't know an area you're going to ride in:
➤ Ask other cyclists about it.
➤ Ride it with a companion.
➤ Examine a map.

Watch for ambush
➤ If a large object blocks your way, turn around quickly. Look for another way to go, or wait until someone else comes by before you pass the object.
➤ Watch buildings, trees, or objects for someone hiding behind them. Swing wide of these wherever you can.
➤ If someone comes at you on the street, ride at them as shown on page 141.
➤ When nearing a possible attacker, pretend you're a cop: Act like you have a radio inside your jacket, and talk into it. Or wear a small speaker or microphone near your shoulder.

Vary your route
If you ride through a bad neighborhood, don't go down the same streets every day at the same time. Bad guys will learn to expect you.

Bridges
Don't ride alone at night on long bridges, like some in New York CIty, San Francisco, and Vancouver. Bad guys can trap you easily.

Learn escape routes
If you ride a road often, look for escape routes. What to think about:
➤ If you're chased by a car, where could you ride (gangways, tunnels, curbs, trees) that a car couldn't?
➤ Can you get somewhere with lots of people around, such as a store, to scare your attacker away?

Act Crazy
If you feel unsafe, act nuts: sing, laugh, shout nonsense, wave your arms and head, drool. You'll seem too unpredictable to mug.

Women: look like a guy
It helps to look male from the rear.
➤ Put your hair up under your helmet. Or tuck your hair inside your jacket and turn your collar up.
➤ Wear loose-fitting clothes.

BEFORE **AFTER**

MOTORIST ADVISORY

BICYCLES BELONG ON THE ROAD!

Traffic rules that apply to motorists also apply to bicyclists.

Because laws in every state and province say bicyclists should act as the drivers of vehicles, motorists should treat them as such. Specifically, motorists should:

➢ Let bicyclists use an entire lane when they have to

➢ Not pull ahead of a bicyclist, then turn in front of them

➢ Pass bicycles with plenty of clearance

➢ At stop signs, yield to bicycles as they would any vehicle

➢ When turning left, yield to oncoming bicycles

➢ Check behind for bicycles before opening a car door

Cyclists should reproduce this message and use it to teach motorists.

Every person propelling a vehicle by human power or riding a bicycle shall have all the rights and all of the duties applicable to the driver of any other vehicle.

Section 11-1202 of the Uniform Vehicle Code

WHAT TO DO

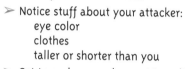

PASSIVE

➤ Don't fight.
➤ Leave your bike and run.
➤ Notice stuff about your attacker:
    eye color
    clothes
    taller or shorter than you
➤ Get to a phone and report to police.

Smart Idea
Don't resist a bad guy who threatens you with a gun or knife. Whatever he wants to take isn't worth your life.

WHEN ATTACKED

VOCAL

➢ Make as much noise as you can.
➢ Scream, yell "thief" and "help," or use a whistle.
➢ Keep making noise until the bad guy is out of sight.

Why?
➢ The bad guy might get scared and run without taking anything.
➢ Other people might notice and capture the bad guy.

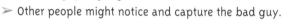

AGGRESSIVE

➢ Carry and use pepper spray (see page 136).
➢ Carry your U lock in your back pocket. If someone comes near you, pull it out and wave it.
(A mini-U lock, like the one shown on page 55, works well for this.)

USING PEPPER

What it does
When sprayed in a person's face, pepper spray makes their eyes burn and water so they can't see. And it makes their nose, mouth, and throat burn so it's hard for them to breathe.

Where to carry
Don't mount the sprayer on your handlebars. You won't have it if a bad guy knocks you off your bike. Carry it on your belt or in your pocket.

How to Practice

1 Go to an outdoor area with no one else around.

2 If it's cold outside, exhale. If the wind is blowing, your breath will go in one direction. Face in that direction.
OR
If it's warm outside, wet your finger and hold it over your head. If the wind is blowing, it'll cool one side of your finger. Face the direction opposite that side.

3 Hold the sprayer at arm's length. Spray for one second. Watch how wide an area the spray covers.

4 Hold the sprayer at arm's length. Spray in a zig-zag pattern for two seconds. Watch how wide an area the spray covers.

SPRAY

You could get busted
A person you spray could charge you with assault. Also, in some places it's a crime to carry pepper spray without a license.

Spraying while on your bike
Don't spray in front of you while riding your bike; it'll blow right into your face. Stop your bike first. If you can, hold one hand slightly in front of the hand holding the spray so the bad guy can't grab the spray.

On your hands
Don't touch the nozzle of the sprayer after you've used it.

Get his shoes
If you disable a bad guy with pepper spray, try to take his shoes. While you're calling police, he won't get as far—and he'll be easier to identify.

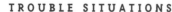

CONFLICTS WITH MOTORISTS

How should you respond to a motorist who hassles you? Some bicyclists follow these three rules:

1. Respond in a way that teaches people the right way to treat bicyclists.

2. Punish the really big jerks.

3. If you can't do (1) or (2) effectively —and in traffic, you usually can't—do nothing.

What about the motorist who really tics you off? Some bicyclists never fight back for a simple reason: A car can really hurt you. Others have a better reason: The motorist you annoy will take it out on the next bicyclist they see.

CONFLICTS WITH PEDESTRIANS

Peds can put you in as much danger as cars. Peds and bicyclists usually look for cars, not each other—so they often surprise each other. But peds usually don't mean you harm. So go easy on them.

CONFLICTS

How to respond to conflicts

Motorist or ped		
Type	**What they do**	
Ignorant	Cut you off because they don't see you or don't think they'll get in your way	
Abusive	Yell or blow their horn at you	
Evil	Hit you with their hand or throw something at you	
Violent	Try to run you down or knock you down	

WHAT TO DO

Nothing

Ignore them. If you have trouble doing this, remember that you don't have to prove you're better than them. *You* are on a *bicycle*.

Smile at those motorists. Remember, you're having a better time than they are.
Karen Mecey
bicycles in Portland OR

WITH MOTORISTS & PEDS

What to do			
page 138	page 139	page 140	page 142
✔	✔		
✔	✔		
✔		✔	✔
		✔	✔

A motorist or pedestrian might hit you some day, if they haven't already. What should you do? It depends on how you want to make them feel. If you plan to get tough, know the best ways to stay out of trouble.

Teach

When the motorist has stopped in traffic, gesture for them to open their window.

EASIEST

Give a printed message
Say, "Can I give this to you?" and hand them a copy of the advisory on page 133. Then ride away.

HARDEST

Tell them what they did wrong
This usually will get you into an argument. But you can try saying one of the following.
"Excuse me, do you know you cut me off back there?"
"Excuse me, why did you blow your horn at me?"
If they get mad, ride away. You've done all you can.

What to do about conflicts: Fight back

Use your fist

1 Do this if you don't have much time to think and you don't want to stop.

2 Smack the hood or side of the car.

3 Another option: Grab the radio antenna and bend it as you go by.

Water to the face

1 While bicycling forward, grab your water bottle and open the nozzle.

2 Hide the bottle behind your back and speed up.

3 When you pass the car's window, squirt your water inside. Don't slow down.

Windshields

A car's windshield is most vulnerable in a spot halfway down and a quarter of the way across, as shown here. **Caution:** If you accidentally hit one of these spots with your U lock or the heel of your gloved hand, you might crack the windshield.

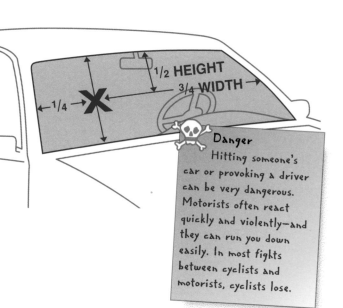

1/2 HEIGHT

3/4 WIDTH →

←1/4→

☠ Danger
Hitting someone's car or provoking a driver can be very dangerous. Motorists often react quickly and violently—and they can run you down easily. In most fights between cyclists and motorists, cyclists lose.

Play chicken

1 Do this if a ped steps out into the street as if to harass you.

2 Speed up in an obvious way. Ride directly at one side of their body.

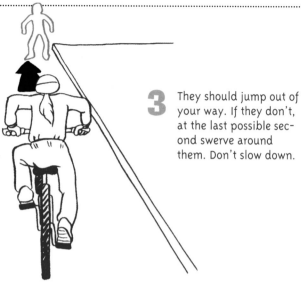

3 They should jump out of your way. If they don't, at the last possible second swerve around them. Don't slow down.

Running from a car

Car can't move forward

➢ Continue straight.
➢ Turn at the first opportunity.

Car chases you across a busy intersection

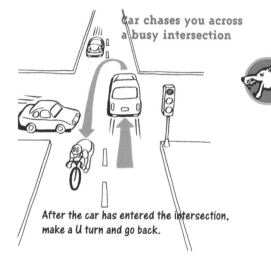

After the car has entered the intersection, make a U turn and go back.

Car is chasing you
Take the sidewalk in the opposite direction.

Someone catches you on foot
➢ Get off of your bike.
➢ Hold it at arm's length between you and them.
➢ If they grab it, let go and run.

What to do about conflicts: Act sly

Sly Bikers only!

Pretend you know them

1 This will confuse many motorists.

2 Smile, wave, and say "Hi, Pat!" Then ride away.

3 This works best if you do it without hesitating. Practice saying "Hi, Pat!" to motorists in traffic. Then when you have to respond to an abusive one—either male or female—you'll say it automatically.

Get legal

1 Notice the car's color, model, and license plate number, and what the motorist and passengers look like. If the incident involved a ped, notice what they wore.

2 When they can no longer see you, stop and write down what you noticed.

3 Go to a phone and call police. Report that you were assaulted.

4 To create more trouble for the motorist: If the incident happens in an area with lots of crime, report that one of the passengers or the ped pointed a gun at you. Rehearse exactly how you'll say this happened, including what the gun looked like.

5 You can also send a warning letter to the motorist's insurance carrier: In some places (such as the state of New York), motor vehicle departments will give you the name and insurer of the person to whom a license plate is registered.

After you've been harassed: how to build up your courage

A motorist who threatens or actually hurts you might really shake you up—so much that you might not want to bike in traffic again. What can you do to build up your courage?

➢ Ride with a companion for the first few days.

➢ If you were harassed on a route you take regularly, take a different route or change the time you leave.

➢ Change things about yourself to make riding feel different. Wear different clothes, or listen to music while you ride.

➢ Carry pepper spray to make you feel more confident. (See page 136.)

If you don't feel safe after a bad experience, don't force yourself to ride. Give yourself time. But when you're ready, get back on that bike . . . don't let the jerks win.

Mary Ellen Paquette
bicycles in Boston

DOGS

Dogs chase bikes every-
where: in cities, suburbs,
and the country. Some dogs
do it just because they like
to chase. Other dogs want to
attack you. When one chases you,
you can't be sure what will work best
(unless you know the dog). Some of
your options are listed here.

STOP HERE AND READ

Just stop
The dog might stop
if you do. If it
does, slowly ride
or walk away.

Stop and get off

1 Stop and get off your bike,
quick.

2 Shout something
commanding, like
"Go home!"

3 If the beast attacks you,
try to keep the bike
between you and it.

Outrun it
This might be a
good idea if there's
more than one dog.

Squirt it
If you try to outrun the dog, a squirt
from your water bottle might slow
Fido down.

Dog repellent

If you continually have a problem with dogs, use a dog-repellent spray. But be careful: wind could blow the stuff back into your face. (See page 136.)

(See page 136.)

Smart Idea
Fill a water bottle with a citrus drink. A squirt from your bottle is less likely to get in your face than a commercial repellent.

Herders

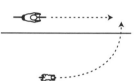

Some dogs in rural areas will instinctively try to herd you: They run at you in an arc, barking. These dogs usually won't hurt you.

Bites

If a dog bites you:

1 Get to a doctor or hospital right away.

2 Report the attack to police.

3 If you can identify the dog, you might avoid a rabies test.

What not to do

Don't outrun it

Don't try to outrun it if you're not sure you can. Many cyclists wipe out when running dogs get caught in their wheels.

Don't hit it

Don't try to hit the dog while riding. You could lose your balance.

EMERGENCY MOVES

When you're riding fast and something gets in your way, should you slam on the brakes? Not always. In emergencies, experienced cyclists use other moves. You can learn them too. Find a quiet parking lot and practice the moves shown on this page.

STOP HERE AND READ

HOW TO SLOW DOWN QUICKLY

The problem
When you stop fast using hand brakes, your weight shifts from the back wheel to the front. On dry pavement, this means pressing hard on your front brake stops you the fastest. What if you press too hard? You'll flip your bike. So you must learn how hard you can apply the front brake.

What to do

1 Find a long (about 1/4 mile) stretch of road where you can practice without interference.

2 Speed up to nearly as fast as you can go.

3 Apply both your front and rear brakes, pressing slightly harder on the front.

front
rear
harder

4 Press harder on your front brake until your back tire starts to skid or lift off the ground. Then ease off of the front brake. You've just found the hardest pressure you can put on it.

5 Repeat but try stopping within shorter and shorter distances. In time, you'll learn how much front braking to use.

Smart Idea
When you have to stop fast, push yourself as far back on the bike as you can. Also put your head and torso as low as you can. This moves some of your weight to the back tire so you don't flip as easily.

☠ **Danger**
Don't use the quick slow-down method on wet pavement. Your front tire will skid and you'll lose control. Instead, apply both brakes evenly. And ride slower!

HOW TO TURN FAST

To make an emergency right turn:

The problem
What do you do when a car turns directly in front of you and you can't brake in time? If you try to turn away you'll wipe out—unless you use this method.

1 You're moving straight, with a car on your left and in front.

2 The car cuts right, in front of you. You steer sharply left, toward the car. This makes you lean right.

3 Turn right hard, steering into the lean and away from the car.

Step 3 follows immediately after step 2. You turn the front wheel left and then right within one second. To make a left turn, reverse the moves.

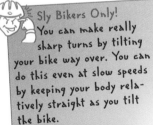

Sly Bikers Only!
You can make really sharp turns by tilting your bike way over. You can do this even at slow speeds by keeping your body relatively straight as you tilt the bike.

HOW TO DODGE A ROCK OR POTHOLE

The problem
Say you're riding down a street, with traffic on your left and parked cars on your right. A pothole appears in front of you. You don't have room to turn left or right. What do you do? Use this dodge.

What to do

1 Just before you reach the obstacle, jerk your front wheel left and then right so it goes around the obstacle.

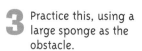

2 Your back tire will also go around the obstacle.

3 Practice this, using a large sponge as the obstacle.

HOW TO FALL

The problem
You usually don't know when you're going to fall, so it's hard to prepare. But here are some things to think about.

When you're about to hit a car, don't try to wipe out first. Down low, you risk going under the wheels or hitting the sharpest parts of the car. Stay upright as long as you can and try to roll.

If you go flying, tuck your head, arms, and legs into a tight ball and try to roll when you hit the ground. If you stick your arms out you're likely to break them, or your collarbone, or both.

Smart Idea
Most serious bicycle injuries involve brain damage. So the best way to protect yourself in a fall is by wearing a helmet. For helmet info, see page 224.

WANT TO PRACTICE FALLING?

1 Wearing thick clothes, gloves, and a helmet, sit on your bike in a field of thick grass.

2 Put both feet on the pedals. Put one pedal at the 6 o'clock position and let the bike fall to that side. Keep your feet on the pedals and hands on the handlebars.

3 Let the outside of your calf absorb the fall first, followed by your thigh, hip, ribs or back, and shoulder. Concentrate on having the fall roll up your body, spreading out the impact.

4 Learn not to stop your fall with your arm, because that's how most cyclists break arms or collarbones.

How to TREAT

1 CLEAN IT RIGHT AWAY
You should clean your wound within the first few minutes. If you don't, dirt and debris will make the wound hurt more and take longer to heal.

2 GET CLEANERS
Use water and a clean piece of fabric, such as your sock. If you're near a restaurant or gas station, go there for soap and napkins.

BEST

Use a clean, stiff hand-scrub brush, bar soap, and water.

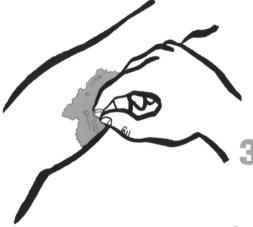

3 PICK OUT GLASS
Pick out any big pieces of glass or other debris.

4 APPLY CLEANERS
Put water on the wound. Put water and soap (if you have it) on the brush or fabric.

A BAD SCRAPE

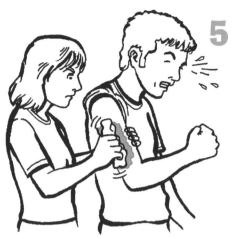

5 SCRUB

Scrub the wound hard for 3 to 5 seconds. More blood will flow, but don't worry—this helps clean the wound.

Scrubbing really hurts—and it should. It works best if somebody scrubs the wound for you. Have them scrub until you finish counting to 10, fast. Counting helps you put up with the pain, because you know when it'll stop.

6 DRY

Pat the wound dry with a clean cloth or napkin.

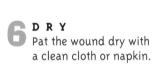

7 BANDAGE

Wrap a clean cloth around the wound. You can tear open one end of a sock and pull it over, or use part of your tights.

BEST

Cover the wound with an antiseptic ointment. Then cover it with an adhesive bandage.

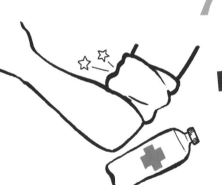

IF YOU CAN'T CLEAN THE WOUND RIGHT AWAY

After you do clean it, put a bag of ice on the wound. Do it for 20 minutes every two hours, until the wound gets less red. If redness and swelling get worse the next day, see a doctor.

SPECIAL TECHNIQUES

Does your bike have multiple gears? If so, maybe you're like a lot people: you don't use 'em. Maybe gears seem too complex to bother with. Or you've gotten along fine without gears, and you can't see why you need them. Well, **this chapter makes gears easy to understand**.

Page 156

Once you've learned about gears, you'll have the power for things like hills, and even stairways. But how do you keep traffic signals from messing up your momentum? **What if you lose control on a downhill?** This chapter has the answers.

Maybe you want to avoid hills, or even heavy traffic. If you don't know local streets well, how do you pick where to ride? This chapter tells you **how to find routes that'll guarantee a nice ride**—instead of urban warfare.

Page 161

Page 172

Bike cops learn how to ride up and down stairs, so there's no reason you can't. But sometimes you'll want to just **carry your bike on stairs**, like when you bring your bike up to your apartment. Or when you take your bike onto escalators at work or the subway station. This stuff is explained step-by-step (get it?) in this chapter.

Page 170

And to where do stairs often lead? Sidewalks. Sure, they're lousy places to ride—too many peds. But sidewalks can come in handy if you want to escape from a chase or beat a traffic light. In this chapter, you can **learn how to use sidewalks** on the sly.

Back on the street, sly bikers use another handy trick: **getting rides from cars**. They get pulled along by a vehicle's air wake—or just grab onto the vehicle itself. Don't try this, kids, without advice from the experts. Get it in this chapter.

Page 165

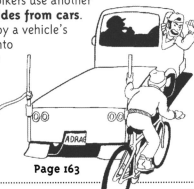

Page 163

WHY YOU NEED MULTIPLE GEARS

Your legs help you go uphill by taking smaller steps or going slower.

Your legs help you go faster by taking bigger steps.

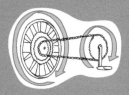

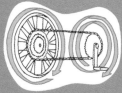

Your bike's gears help you go uphill or start from a stop by having you pedal faster, yet more easily.

New Word

Cadence

How fast you pedal, or the number of times your pedals go around in one minute. Your legs will not get as tired if you can keep a steady cadence all the time. This means that you pedal at the same speed—whether you're going fast or slow, uphill or downhill.

STEADY PACE ON A HILL

You're going very fast, using a small back gear.

As you start to go up a hill, you move slower. Your pedals will move slower too—unless you shift to a bigger back gear to keep them moving at the same speed.

In the middle of the hill climb, you move even slower. You shift to the biggest back gear to keep your pedals moving at a steady speed.

STEADY PACE WHILE STARTING

When you start from a stop, you move slowly. You use the biggest back gear so your pedals don't move slowly.

As you move faster, you shift to a smaller back gear so your pedals don't also move faster.

STEADY PACE INTO A WIND

You're going very fast, using a small back gear.

As you start to go into the wind, you move slower. Your pedals will move slower too—unless you shift to a bigger back gear to keep them moving at the same speed.

GEARS

In the middle of the downhill, you move fastest. You shift to the smallest back gear to keep your pedals moving at a steady speed.

At the top of the hill you start to move faster. You shift to a smaller back gear so your pedals don't also move faster.

 STOP HERE AND READ

Whenever you want to walk up a hill or go from walking to running, your legs move differently. Your steps become shorter or longer. That's how your legs adapt to the different kind of work you want to do. Your bike also can adapt, if it has multiple gears. It adapts by changing gears. By changing gears, you can move faster, go uphill, or ride upwind without working so hard.

& STOPPING

When you're moving the fastest, you shift to the smallest back gear to keep your pedals moving at a steady speed.

As you brake to slow down, you shift to a bigger back gear so your pedals don't also slow down.

As you come to a stop, you shift to your biggest back gear so it's already engaged when you start again.

When the wind hits you the strongest, you move even slower. You shift to the biggest back gear to keep your pedals moving at a steady speed.

As the wind dies down you start to move faster. You shift to a smaller back gear so your pedals don't also move faster.

How HAND SHIFTERS

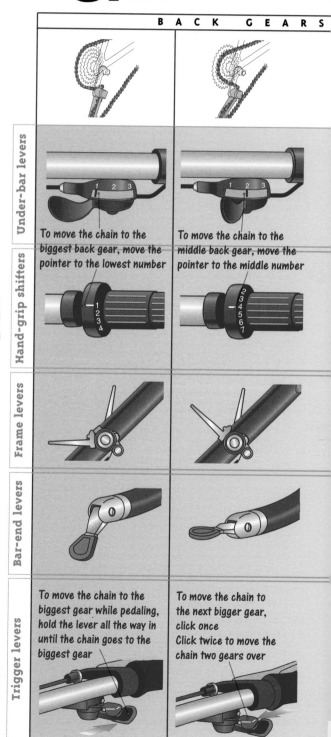

B A C K   G E A R S

STOP HERE AND READ

Most multi-geared bikes have either external or internal gears (see p. 158). No matter which kind your bike has, your bike's hand shifters make the bike shift gears. To shift gears on some bikes, you simply move the hand shifter up or down slightly. On other bikes, the hand shifter acts like a trigger: You push it, it clicks, then it returns to its original position. These pages show you how different hand shifters cause your bike to shift gears.

HOW TO TELL WHAT GEAR YOU'RE ON

With most frame and bar-end levers, there's only one way to tell which back gear the chain is on: look down at the gear. Some levers help you, though: they make a clicking noise each time you change to a new gear. What if your levers don't click? Whenever you want to change gears, move the lever slowly until your pedaling feels easier or harder, and the chain doesn't make a rattling noise. See page 158 for details.

Under-bar levers

To move the chain to the biggest back gear, move the pointer to the lowest number

To move the chain to the middle back gear, move the pointer to the middle number

Hand-grip shifters

Frame levers

Bar-end levers

Trigger levers

To move the chain to the biggest gear while pedaling, hold the lever all the way in until the chain goes to the biggest gear

To move the chain to the next bigger gear, click once
Click twice to move the chain two gears over

CHANGE GEARS

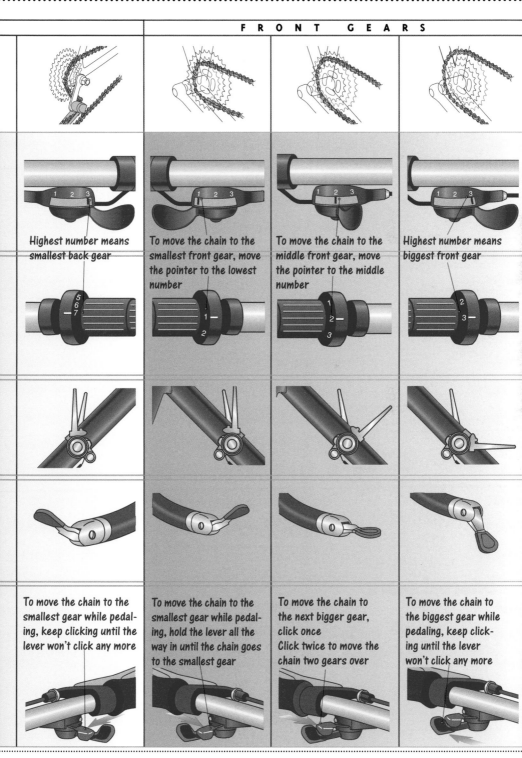

Highest number means smallest back gear

To move the chain to the smallest front gear, move the pointer to the lowest number

To move the chain to the middle front gear, move the pointer to the middle number

Highest number means biggest front gear

To move the chain to the smallest gear while pedaling, keep clicking until the lever won't click any more

To move the chain to the smallest gear while pedaling, hold the lever all the way in until the chain goes to the smallest gear

To move the chain to the next bigger gear, click once
Click twice to move the chain two gears over

To move the chain to the biggest gear while pedaling, keep clicking until the lever won't click any more

How to SHIFT

External gears

The back wheel or front wheel (or both) has two or more gears attached to its side. Moving a hand shifter pulls or pushes a *derailleur*, which makes the bike's chain move to a different gear.

1 **To shift:** Pedal with very little pressure.

2 Move the hand shifter. If it clicks once for each gear, move the shifter until it clicks. If it doesn't click, move it slowly until your pedaling becomes easier or harder, or you hear the chain move to another gear.

3 If your chain rattles or rubs after you've shifted, move the shifter until the sound is gone. If the sound remains, have your bike checked.

Back gears

Use the biggest gear when you go the slowest.

Use the next-to-biggest gears when you go a little faster.

Use the smallest gear when you go the fastest.

Use the next-to-smallest gears when you go moderately fast.

Some bikes have as many as ten back gears.

Situation	Do this
You're learning how to shift gears.	Stay in a single front gear. Learn to use back gears before you start shifting the front gears.
You're speeding downhill and want to keep pedaling at a steady pace, or you want to go faster without pedaling faster; and you've shifted to your smallest back gear.	Shift to a bigger front gear.
You're climbing a hill or going into the wind; you've shifted to your biggest back gear; and you want to pedal more easily.	Shift to a smaller front gear.

Internal gears

➢ The hub of the back wheel contains three or more gears. Moving the shifter connects a different gear to the wheel.
➢ Use lower-numbered gears for slow speeds, headwinds, and uphills. Use higher numbers for the opposite.

To shift:

1 While the bike moves forward, stop pedaling.

2 Move the shifter to the number of the gear you want. Then start pedaling.

BUMPS & RUTS

Riding across a bump

1 Just before the front wheel hits the bump, take most of your weight off of the handle-bars, and make your arms loose.

2 Just before the back wheel hits the bump, take most of your weight off of the seat. For a large bump, take your butt off of the seat completely.

Riding on rough pavement

Take your butt off of the seat.

Keep your arms and legs flexible to absorb the shaking.

Shift most of your weight to your pedals.

Riding through holes

1 Just before the front wheel hits the far side of the hole, take most of your weight off of the handlebars so your front wheel comes up easily.

2 Before the back wheel hits the hole, take your butt off of the seat and lean forward. The back wheel should roll through the hole.

Crossing railroad tracks

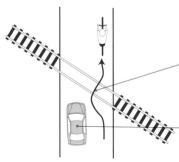

To keep your tires from catching in ruts next to diagonal railroad tracks, change your approach so you cross the tracks at a right angle.

Before you swerve, check for traffic in your path.

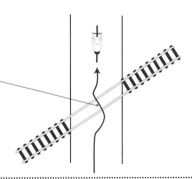

HILLS

Going Uphill

If your uphill route includes traffic lights, learn to time the lights: Don't start up the hill until you know you'll pass the light when it's green, so you don't have to stop.

If your uphill route includes a stop sign, try to shadow a car through the intersection: Time your arrival at the stop sign so you can go through the intersection at the same time as an oncoming or following car, so you don't have to stop.

1 Speed up before you get to the hill, to give you more momentum. Try to go fast enough to get into your highest gear.

5 If you slow down to an uncomfortable pace, stand up while pedaling.

Grease in a parking lane can make you slip. Keep an eye on traffic behind you in case you have to swerve.

4 Don't just push down with your forward pedal; when each foot reaches the bottom of its stroke, pull it back and up.

3 Downshift only as far as you need to keep the speed of your pedaling constant.

2 As you start to climb, stay in your highest gear until your pedaling starts to slow. Don't stop pedaling.

Going Downhill

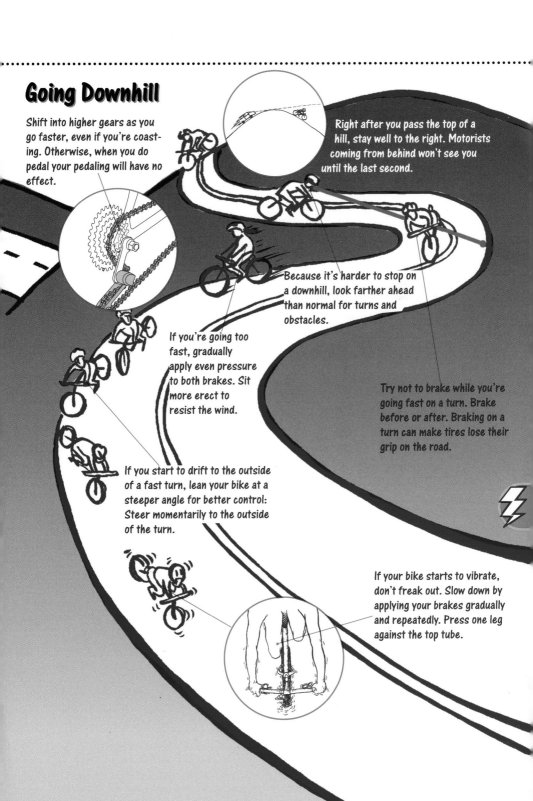

Shift into higher gears as you go faster, even if you're coasting. Otherwise, when you do pedal your pedaling will have no effect.

Right after you pass the top of a hill, stay well to the right. Motorists coming from behind won't see you until the last second.

Because it's harder to stop on a downhill, look farther ahead than normal for turns and obstacles.

If you're going too fast, gradually apply even pressure to both brakes. Sit more erect to resist the wind.

Try not to brake while you're going fast on a turn. Brake before or after. Braking on a turn can make tires lose their grip on the road.

If you start to drift to the outside of a fast turn, lean your bike at a steeper angle for better control: Steer momentarily to the outside of the turn.

If your bike starts to vibrate, don't freak out. Slow down by applying your brakes gradually and repeatedly. Press one leg against the top tube.

CATCHING A

How to draft

IDEAL

Van with rear windows. You can see what's coming, so you know when the van might slow or stop.

Sly Bikers Only
Drafting is the act of following a big, fast vehicle very closely so its air wake pulls you along. Why draft? It helps when you're riding uphill or into a head wind—or you just want to go fast.

NOT AS GOOD

Bus or truck. Stay close to the right side so you can watch ahead.

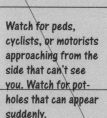

Watch for peds, cyclists, or motorists approaching from the side that can't see you. Watch for potholes that can appear suddenly.

Danger
When you follow a vehicle closely, you have to keep watching the pavement directly in front of you. If a pothole appears, you'll have only a split second to dodge it—far less time than you'd have if you spotted it way in advance. See page 66 for road-scanning methods, and page 159 for riding across bumps.

Smart Idea
Don't move too far to the side, or you'll fall out of the vehicle's wake and slow down. If this happens, immediately move back toward the middle while you try to catch up.

RIDE FROM A VEHICLE

How to skitch

The first few times you skitch, practice on very large trucks. They don't speed up or slow down as quickly as smaller vehicles. Or practice with a friend's truck, going slowly.

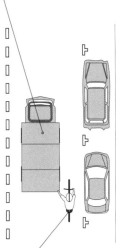

Two reasons to ride at the vehicle's right rear:
- You can watch for something that might cause the vehicle to slow. If an obstacle appears you can duck left.
- If the vehicle slows suddenly, you can let go and continue straight.

The best way to grab the vehicle is with an open grip. Why? When your fingers are hooked around something, it takes a second longer to let go. And if the vehicle does something unexpected, you might need that second. Also, if you panic you might clench your fingers—which means you'd take even longer to let go.

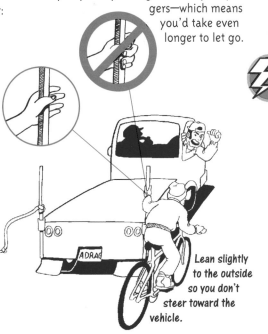

Lean slightly to the outside so you don't steer toward the vehicle.

USING SIDEWALKS

Sidewalks can slow you down. Pedestrians (peds) belong there more than you do; take care not to hit peds, cut them off, or freak them out. (On sidewalks, bikes are real dangerous to seniors and kids.) But sidewalks can help you pass jammed traffic, dodge a swerving car, or run from a nasty motorist conflict. If you use sidewalks a lot, learn where to find curb cuts or how to jump curbs without hurting your wheels.

Jumping onto a curb: the foot method

1 Approach the curb at a 45-degree angle or less. Put the curb-side pedal into the lowest (6 o'clock) position.

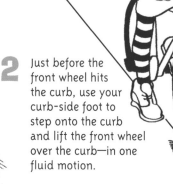

2 Just before the front wheel hits the curb, use your curb-side foot to step onto the curb and lift the front wheel over the curb—in one fluid motion.

Shortcuts

When a traffic jam blocks the street, watch for clear stretches of sidewalk that'll help you quickly bypass the jam.

BIG LUG MOVERS

If your bike has thin tires, look for curb cuts or driveways through which to get on and off the sidewalk.

New Word
Curb cut
A curb cut is a place where the sidewalk is level with the street. That is, the curb has been cut out and the sidewalk made into a ramp. Towns usually make curb cuts to accommodate wheelchairs and strollers.

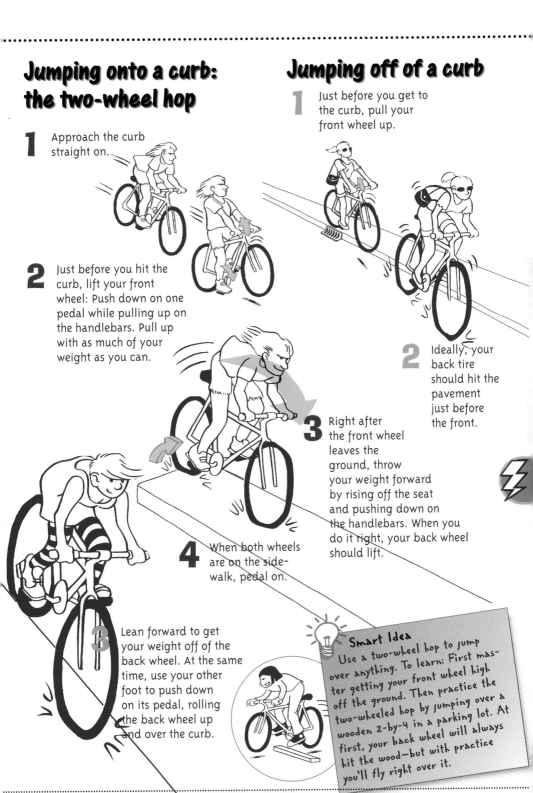

Jumping onto a curb: the two-wheel hop

1 Approach the curb straight on.

2 Just before you hit the curb, lift your front wheel: Push down on one pedal while pulling up on the handlebars. Pull up with as much of your weight as you can.

3 Lean forward to get your weight off of the back wheel. At the same time, use your other foot to push down on its pedal, rolling the back wheel up and over the curb.

4 When both wheels are on the sidewalk, pedal on.

Jumping off of a curb

1 Just before you get to the curb, pull your front wheel up.

2 Ideally, your back tire should hit the pavement just before the front.

3 Right after the front wheel leaves the ground, throw your weight forward by rising off the seat and pushing down on the handlebars. When you do it right, your back wheel should lift.

Smart Idea
Use a two-wheel hop to jump over anything. To learn: First master getting your front wheel high off the ground. Then practice the two-wheeled hop by jumping over a wooden 2-by-4 in a parking lot. At first, your back wheel will always hit the wood—but with practice you'll fly right over it.

CARRYING

If there's no one on the elevator,
roll the bike straight on.

Immediately turn the bike around and
hold it against a side wall.

If there are people on the elevator,
ask the people on one side to move
to the middle. Then stand your bike up
as shown on page 167.

Roll the bike onto the elevator and
go to the side wall. When you get
off, back out.

Two ways to go up stairs

1 Reach over the top of the bike and grab the seat-post tube on the lowest part. Grab the handlebars near the middle. Lift the bike and walk up the stairs.

2 Bend at your knees so that your shoulder is level with the bike's top tube. With your elbow bent, grab the top tube from underneath, close to the seat.

Grab the handlebars near the middle. Holding your bent arm steady, stand up—hoisting the bike near your shoulder. Carry the bike up the stairs.

Smart Idea
Does your seat hit low ceilings on stairways? Install a quick-release bolt so you can remove the seat before climbing stairs. (And when you park your bike outside, take your seat with you.)

166

BIKES ON STAIRS

Three ways to go down stairs

1 Stand over your rear wheel.
Grab the handlebars.
Pull back and stand the bike up.
Roll the bike down the stairs.

2 Reach over the top of
the bike and grab the
seat-post tube on the
lowest part. Grab the
handlebars near the
middle. Carry or roll
the bike down the
stairs.

3 Bend at your knees so that
your shoulder is level with
the bike's top tube. With
your elbow bent, grab the
top tube from underneath,
close to the seat. Grab the
handlebars near the middle.

Holding your bent
arm steady, stand up—
hoisting the bike near
your shoulder. Carry
the bike down the stairs.

Recommended Product
Shoulder pads
Several manufacturers make triangular pads that attach underneath your top tube, so you can comfortably carry your bike on your shoulder. Most of these products double as a carrying pack. And most pads double as storage pouches, inside of which you can carry stuff. (For more on Mr. Bike's Recommended Products, go to www.mrbike.com/products.)

Bikes on

Going up

1 Stand on the right side of your bike, with your right hand on the right side of the handlebars, and your left hand holding the back of the seat.

8 Roll the bike forward as your left foot steps off.

2 Roll the front wheel onto the bottom stair (stair #1). Press forward slightly so the wheel stays against the back of the preceding stair.

7 Let go of the brake as your right foot steps off of the escalator.

3 Put your right foot on stair #2, still pressing the bike forward gently.

6 At the top of the escalator, let the front wheel roll off of the stair.

4 Put your left foot onto stair #3 and let your rear wheel roll onto the same stair.

5 Apply the rear brake firmly. The rear brake keeps the bike from rolling back.

ESCALATORS

Going down

1 Stand on the left side of your bike, with your left hand on the left side of the handlebars, and your right hand holding the front of the seat.

9 As your right foot steps off of the escalator, roll the bike forward.

2 Roll the front wheel onto the top stair (stair #1)

8 Step off of the escalator with your left foot.

3 Apply the front brake firmly as you put your left foot on stair #2. The front brake keeps your bike from rolling forward.

7 Let the front wheel roll off of the stair.

4 Put your right foot on stair #3.

6 At the bottom of the escalator, release the front brake as the front wheel touches the floor. Hold the seat firmly so the bike doesn't get away from you.

5 Let your rear wheel roll onto stair #3.

Riding up stairs

1 Shift into a low enough speed (with the chain on a big back gear) so you can pedal uphill.

2 Put your pedals at the 3 and 9 o'clock positions and stand up on them. Move your butt back so most of your weight is toward the back of the bike.

Keep your knees and elbows flexible so they can absorb the bumps.

3 Just before the first stair, pull your front wheel up. You should raise it high enough so that it lands on the second stair.

4 When your front wheel lands on the stair, start pedaling. Keep your weight back—or else your front wheel will slam to a stop. Pedal up the stairs.

5 When your front wheel reaches the top landing, shift your weight forward. Continue pedaling as your back wheel reaches the top.

STAIRS

Riding down stairs

1 Shift to your biggest front and back gears so your chain has maximum tension. Otherwise, it might jump off of the gears.

Approach the stairs straight on. Even the slightest angle could make you lose control.

STOP HERE AND READ

When someone's chasing you, especially from a car, stairways can make for a good escape. Sure, you could always stop, get off of your bike, carry it over the stairs, and hop back on. But getting on and off of your bike takes time—time you won't need if you get good at stair-hopping as shown on this page. Practice on small stairways, ones with two to four steps.

2 Just before the first stair, put your pedals at the 3 and 9 o'clock positions and stand up on them. Move your butt back so most of your weight is toward the back of the bike.

Hold the handlebars tightly, with a couple of fingers over your back brake lever.

3 As your bike starts down the stairs, keep your knees and elbows flexible so they can absorb the bumps. Keep your weight back.

4 Use only your back brake to slow down. If you go too slow, you'll have a very rough ride. On long stairways you can go fast enough to get a rhythm, so that both wheels appear to be hopping the stairs at the same time.

5 When your back wheel hits the bottom, start pedaling. If your going fast enough, immediately shift to a faster gear.

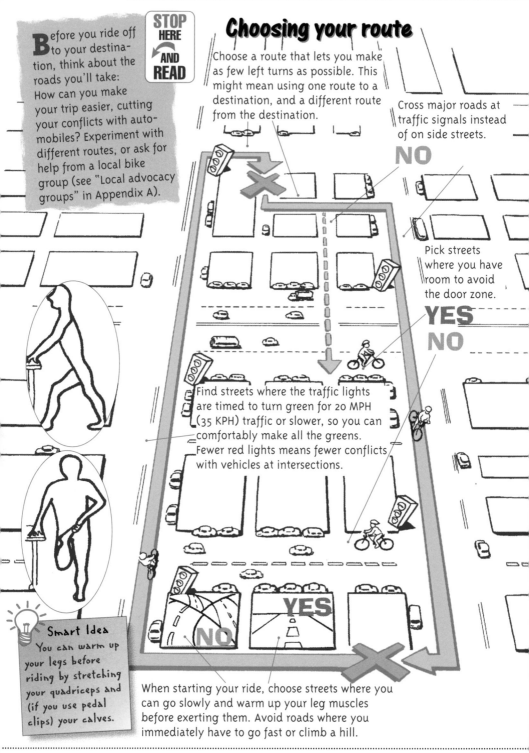

Before you ride off to your destination, think about the roads you'll take: How can you make your trip easier, cutting your conflicts with automobiles? Experiment with different routes, or ask for help from a local bike group (see "Local advocacy groups" in Appendix A).

Choosing your route

Choose a route that lets you make as few left turns as possible. This might mean using one route to a destination, and a different route from the destination.

Cross major roads at traffic signals instead of on side streets.

NO

Pick streets where you have room to avoid the door zone.

YES
NO

Find streets where the traffic lights are timed to turn green for 20 MPH (35 KPH) traffic or slower, so you can comfortably make all the greens. Fewer red lights means fewer conflicts with vehicles at intersections.

YES

NO

Smart Idea
You can warm up your legs before riding by stretching your quadriceps and (if you use pedal clips) your calves.

When starting your ride, choose streets where you can go slowly and warm up your leg muscles before exerting them. Avoid roads where you immediately have to go fast or climb a hill.

WAY

Choosing street maps

STOP HERE AND READ

Maps are good tools to help you figure out how to get around town on your bike. But some maps will help you more than others. Even one that carries the name "bicycling map" might not work as well as a standard street map. Here's what to look for.

OK

Bike routes with no street detail
Shows only recommended bike routes or streets with marked bike lanes, but few or no other street names. OK if you know streets well.

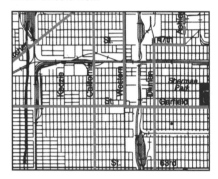

GOOD

Bike routes with street detail
Shows all the streets and their names, along with recommended bike routes or marked bike lanes.

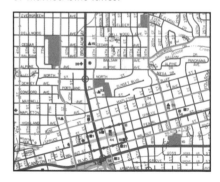

OK

Street detail
Shows all the streets and their names. OK if you don't need bike-route suggestions.

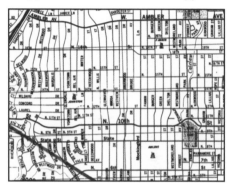

BEST

Bike routes, street detail, extras
Shows all streets names, bike routes, and helpful info such as: one-way designations; elevation (for hilly areas); bike parking locations; high-traffic volume.

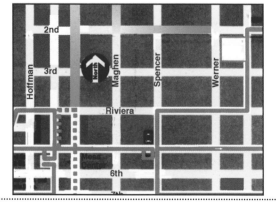

BUSES, TRAINS, & PLANES

7

Lots of cities have **bike-carrying racks on transit buses**. Bicyclists have learned a few tricks for putting bikes onto these racks. And, where buses don't have racks, cyclists have tricks for taking bikes inside of buses. They're all in this chapter, along with step-by-step instructions.

Page 181

Most cities publish their own bike-on-bus rack instructions. But they don't tell you how **the racks might screw up your commute**. Luckily, cyclists across the country have learned—and they tell you in this chapter.

Page 182

Taking your bike onto a subway or light rail is even trickier. Where's the best place to put yourself? How do you keep your bike from getting thrown around? And what do you do on a crowded car? This chapter gives you the answers.

Page 187

Commuter trains are a little different from subways. Conductors, special placement areas, stairs, and schedules can trip you up. But not if you look at this chapter.

Page 191

Page 200

Hey, what if someone told you bikes can fly? Nuts, you'd say—and you'd almost be right. **Getting your bike into an airport and onto a plane** can make you crazy. But many cyclists have done it. Their sanity-saving hints are in this chapter.

BIKES ON

Many cities have installed bike-carrying racks on the front of their transit buses. Why use them? If you have a very long commute or must travel through a bike-restricted area, you can ride the bus partway. Also, if rain catches you unprepared or you get a flat you can't fix, you can hop the bus. Once you learn how, using a bike-on-bus rack is easy.

Timing

Most bike-on-bus racks carry only two bikes. So by the time a bus gets to your stop, the rack might be full—so you have to wait for the next bus. What to do if you commute regularly:

1 The first couple of weeks, leave your house much earlier than usual so you won't be late. After that if you haven't had a problem with full racks, try leaving a little later each day—until you find the best time to leave.

2 Experiment with different bus routes that go in your direction. Your bike gives you the flexibility to take any of several parallel routes.

Smart Idea
In some places you need a permit to put your bike on a bus. Before you plan your first trip, learn how long it takes to get the permit, and where to get it.

Don't forget!
Many bus riders forget their bikes are on the bus! If you've regularly ridden the bus before you started bringing your bike, make yourself a reminder—such as hanging your helmet on your arm.

Watch
Stay near the front of the bus and watch your bike. A two-person thief team can distract a driver while stealing your bike. Or a dishonest cyclist might take your bike and leave you their junk. To deter thieves, lock one wheel before loading your bike.

BUSES: BASICS

Learn
Call your transit agency for a route map, schedule, and list of rules—including times that bikes aren't allowed. Learn the routes on which bikes are allowed. Also ask for bike-on-bus brochures or videos.

Practice
Before you use a bike-on-bus rack for the first time, practice on a real bus. Bring your bike to where a bus is waiting at its origin or turnaround point. Ask the driver to let you try the rack.

Relax
The first few times you rack your bike, you'll think you're taking too long. Relax. View yourself not as a cyclist, but as a passenger with a bike; you're just as entitled to a little extra time as a passenger with heavy groceries or a wheelchair.

Smart Idea
Ask your transit agency to hold public training in which they teach people how to use bike-on-bus racks.

LOADING A

No bikes already loaded

1 Take bags or other big accessories off of your bike and lay them on the sidewalk.

2 When a bus approaches, stand with your bike so that the driver can see it.

11 Grab any stuff you'd left on the sidewalk and board the bus.

10 Shake your bike to make sure it's secure.

9 Pull the support arm out, up, and over your front tire to about the 11 o'clock position. If the tire has a fender, put the arm just below it.

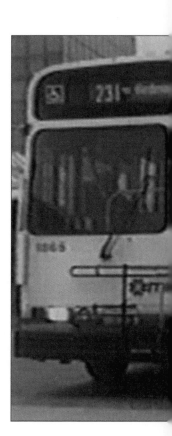

FRONT BUS RACK

3 When the bus stops, walk with your bike on your right side to the middle of the front of the bus, about three feet away.

4 Holding your bike with your right hand, use your left hand to pull the rack down.

5 Move your bike between you and the rack.

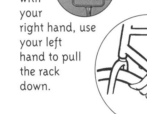

6 Grab your bike with your left hand on the wheel and down tube, and your right hand in the middle of the seat tube.

8 Holding the bike with your right hand, grab the rack's support arm with your left hand.

7 Lift the bike onto the wheel well farthest from you.

When no bikes are already in the rack, some agencies require you to put your bike on the outer wheel well.

Bike already loaded

1 Take bags or other big accessories off of your bike and lay them on the sidewalk.

2 When a bus approaches, stand with your bike so that the driver can see it.

9 Grab any stuff you'd left on the sidewalk and board the bus.

8 Shake your bike to make sure it's secure.

3 When the bus stops, walk with your bike on your left side to the middle of the front of the rack. If loading to the inner side: Back your bike to the rack's left side.

4 Grab your bike with one hand on the wheel and down tube, and the other hand in the middle of the seat tube.

5 Lift the bike onto the wheel well closest to you.

6 Holding the bike with one hand, grab the rack's support arm with your other hand.

7 Pull the support arm out, up, and over your front tire to about the 1 o'clock position. If the tire has a fender, put the arm just below it.

Removing your bike

1 Tell the driver you'll be removing your bike at the next stop.

2 Get off the bus at the front door. Place anything you're carrying on the sidewalk.

3 Stand in front of your front tire and pull the support arm out and down.

4 Grab your bike with one hand on the wheel and down tube, and the other hand in the middle of the seat tube.

5 Lift your bike out of the wheel well. If there's another bike on the rack, carry or roll your bike onto the sidewalk.

☠ **Danger**
Don't step out to the traffic side of the bus.

6 If there is no other bike on the rack, place the bike on the ground next to you and hold it with one hand. With the other hand, fold the rack up against the front of the bus. Then roll your bike onto the sidewalk.

Bikes Inside Buses

Slim your bike
Some bus doorways have railings that you and your bike can squeeze through, but not with side bags. Buses can have narrow aisles, too. Before you board such a bus, remove your bags and put them onto the floor of the bus. Then carry your bike on.

Pay later
On a moving bus, it's hard to fish out your fare money while holding a bike. If your bus agency doesn't have rules to guide you, do this: When you board, ask the driver if you can first secure your bike, then pay your fare.

Get a transfer
On some buses you put your bike in the space reserved for wheelchairs. If no wheelchair is already there, you can board with your bike. But if a passenger using a wheelchair boards after you, they can bump you off the bus. For this reason, when you board the bus, get a transfer (if your system has them) so you don't have to pay for the next bus.

Carry bungees
Some buses require you to tie your bike so it doesn't move around. For this purpose, always carry at least two 14-inch bungee cords.

Stand it up
If you share the space with many passengers, stand your bike up on its rear wheel. See page 189 for tips on how to secure it.

STOP HERE AND READ

Some cities' buses don't have outside racks, but you may bring your bike on board. Also, in a couple of places where bike-on-bus racks block the buses' headlights, after dark you must carry your bike inside the bus. Here are some tips for doing so.

Smart idea
Know your bike. It has sharp edges that can cut someone, and a greasy chain that can soil their clothes. Warn passengers who get too close.

Getting on

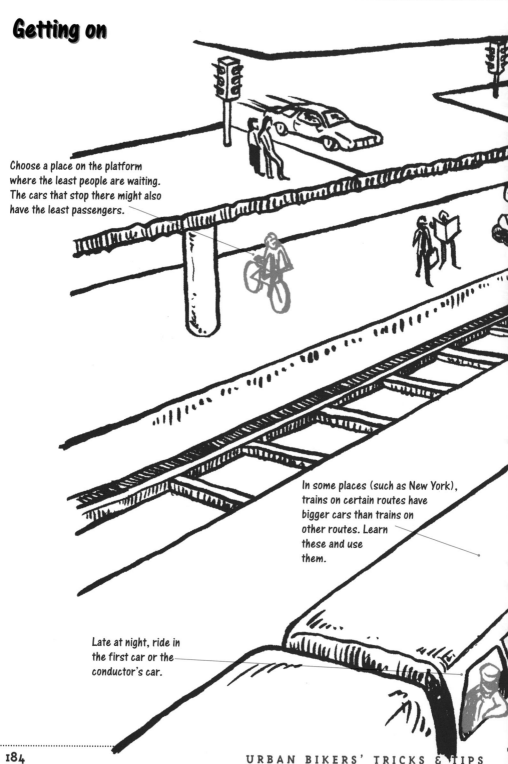

Choose a place on the platform where the least people are waiting. The cars that stop there might also have the least passengers.

In some places (such as New York), trains on certain routes have bigger cars than trains on other routes. Learn these and use them.

Late at night, ride in the first car or the conductor's car.

LIGHT RAIL

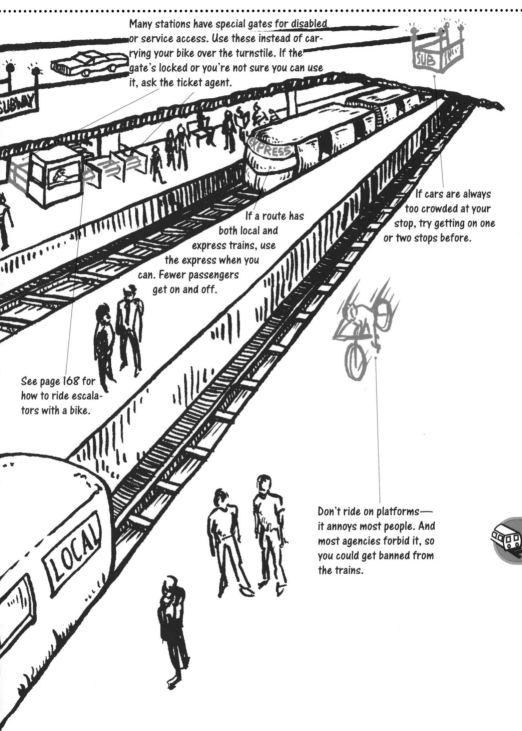

Many stations have special gates for disabled or service access. Use these instead of carrying your bike over the turnstile. If the gate's locked or you're not sure you can use it, ask the ticket agent.

If a route has both local and express trains, use the express when you can. Fewer passengers get on and off.

If cars are always too crowded at your stop, try getting on one or two stops before.

See page 168 for how to ride escalators with a bike.

Don't ride on platforms— it annoys most people. And most agencies forbid it, so you could get banned from the trains.

Placing your bike

If your town has rules about exactly where on a subway car bikes should go, follow the rules if they seem practical. But try to put your bike where it blocks the fewest people who want to sit down or move through the car. Unused doorways are best because your bike's completely out of the way.

STOP HERE AND READ

Put your bike in the middle next to a center pole, especially if all seats are taken. Lean your bike against the pole.

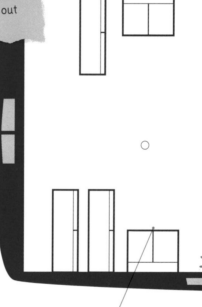

Sit in the aisle-facing seat next to the door, with your bike in front of you. A small part of the wheel can stick out into the doorway.

➢ If your bike has a kickstand, face the kickstand side of the bike toward the seat and put the kick-stand down. Warn passengers not to rub against your chain.

➢ If your bike has no kickstand, face the chain side of the bike toward the seat. Sit down and lean the bike against your knees.

Smart idea
Know your bike. It has sharp edges that can cut someone, and a greasy chain that can soil their clothes. Warn passengers who get too close.

If, when the train stops, doors open only on one side, place your bike in a doorway on the other side. If door openings alternate from side to side, you can move from side one to the other—if the car's not crowded.

Put your bike in the wheelchair space. Plan where you'd put your bike next if a wheelchair boards the car.

If there are few passengers, take a seat and put your bike next to you.

With many passengers present, put your bike in the back or front of the car, especially at either end of the train. Stand it up or put it across the door. Get ready to move it if someone comes through the door.

Don't try to get on a packed subway car at rush hour. You'll make enemies for other cyclists. If you keep encountering crowds, change your commute time.

Holding your bike

When sitting with your bike leaned against your knees, place each foot next to the wheel so the bike won't roll in either direction.

Lean the bike against the door, sit on the top tube, and hold one brake lever.

☠ **Danger**
Don't lean against or block a door unless you're sure it won't open at an upcoming stop.

💡 **Smart Idea**
The more you lean your bike the less likely it will roll.

Lock or bungee your bike to a pole. Don't do this on short rides, or if train rules don't allow it.

Stand the bike up and hang it from an overhead pole. Place an S hook through the front tire and over the pole. (For suppliers, see "Hardware" in Appendix B.)

Make sure rear-mounted stuff won't fall off.

Make sure the chain faces away from other passengers.

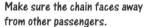

Hold the bike with its brakes on: To keep the brake on without holding the lever, use a Velcro ankle strap, your bike glove strap, or something (such as a coin) jammed into the brake lever.

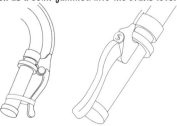

If your bike doesn't have a kickstand and you use the train often, get one. With a kickstand, you can more easily support a bike's weight. (But some train rules don't let you put your kick stand down!)

COMMUTER TRAINS
BASICS

Permits

When applying for a permit, get one for each member of your family. (If you don't have a family, make one up). Then, when your bicycling friends visit from out of town, you can all bring your bikes onto the train. (This

won't work on trains that have photographic permits.) And if permits expire annually, don't forget to renew them.

STOP HERE AND READ

Many cities allow bikes on commuter trains. Some require you to have a permit. Others let you board with a bike only at certain times or in certain cars. But even where you're allowed to board with a bike, you might get discouraged by lack of room, other passengers, or rail employees. Don't. Be polite, but firm—you belong there! Above all, be creative: Bungee cords can help you stow your bike almost anywhere on a train.

Split routes

Be careful with train routes in which you have to change trains. The second train might not accommodate your bike because it's smaller or configured differently.

Conductors

➢ As long as conductors let your bike on the train, don't argue with them or get them mad—even if they don't follow the rules exactly. On the train, they're the bosses. Don't make enemies for other cyclists.

➢ A certain train might have just started carrying bikes. Or its passengers might seldom board with bikes. So to its conductors, passengers with bikes are a new thing. On such a train, ask conductors where they want you to put your bike. They might not know themselves, but your respect will help other cyclists.

➢ If a conductor mistakenly stops you from boarding with a bike: Note the time of the train and the conductor's name, if you can get it. If you can't, write down a description of the conductor and which car they were on. Then report the incident to the transit agency and the local bike advocacy group.

GETTING OFF A TRAIN

Get ready

At the stop before yours, start preparing to get off. Untie your bike and attach any accessories you removed.

Yield

Let passengers without bikes get off the train first, unless you'll block them.

Getting out

If you have bags on your bike that won't fit through the door, put your bags on the floor near the stairs.

Carry your bike out the door and lean it against the train. Immediately run back for your bags.

BIKES ON

Tying to wall mounts

1 Put one hook of the bungee on the wall mount.

2 Run the bungee through one wheel so the bike won't roll.

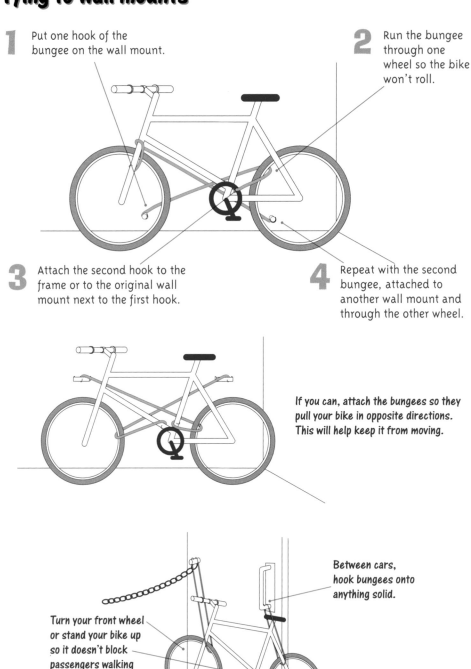

3 Attach the second hook to the frame or to the original wall mount next to the first hook.

4 Repeat with the second bungee, attached to another wall mount and through the other wheel.

If you can, attach the bungees so they pull your bike in opposite directions. This will help keep it from moving.

Between cars, hook bungees onto anything solid.

Turn your front wheel or stand your bike up so it doesn't block passengers walking between cars.

Wall-mounted racks

When leaning your bike against a bike already attached to a wall-mounted rack, face it in the opposite direction. Its handlebars won't get in the way.

Don't jam your pedal into the other bike's wheels.

Your trains might have areas where the seats have been removed. In some cities these spaces are made just for bikes. In other cities these spaces are made for wheelchairs—but if they're empty, bikes can use them. On other trains, no seats have been removed but bikes are allowed between cars.

Smart idea
Put a sign on your bike that shows the name of the stop at which you're getting off.

Before attaching your bike against another bike, ask its owner where he or she is getting off. (Call out "Where's this bike going?") If you're getting off later, you may want to put the earlier-departing bike on the outside.

GOTTA HAVE BUNGEES

You can't lash your bike to the wall of a train without bungee cords. A few trains contain racks with bungees already attached—but you should always have at least two of your own. Get bungees that are at least 24 inches long when they're not stretched.

Where bikes sit separately from passengers, sit where you can watch your bike—because sometimes bikes on trains get stolen.

Smart idea
To prevent theft, hobble your bike: lock the front wheel to the frame.

TRAIN TRAVEL

Timing your commute

No room

Some trains carry a limited number of bikes. So by the time a train gets to your stop, it might already have the maximum number. What to do if you commute regularly:

1. The first couple of weeks, leave home much earlier than usual so you won't be late. After that, if you haven't had a problem with full trains, try leaving a little later each day—until you find the best time to leave.

2. Try bicycling to a station before the one you usually use.

Flex time

If your commuter train doesn't allow bikes during rush hours, ask your boss for flex time: you could work from 7 a.m to 3 p.m., or from 10 a.m. to 6 p.m.

Work early, home late

Say your commuter train doesn't allow bikes during rush hours. If you leave home earlier and go home later, you can use the extra time to eat breakfast and dinner: Bring food with you and eat away from home. Don't eat on a train unless you know whether food's allowed.

Sports crowds

Certain trains pass close to sports stadiums. When big sports games are over, these trains get swamped with passengers. Learn when games end so you can avoid the nearby trains.

Traveling between cities

Amtrak trains in the U.S. and Via Rail trains in Canada have different ways of handling bikes. Most make you put your bike in a box and check it as baggage. Others, such as Amtrak's Cascades, Piedmont, and Downeasters have cars with bike racks; you just roll your bike on. (To learn how to pack your bike into a box, see page 202.)

Amtrak's National Timetable tells you which trains take checked baggage at which stops. Also, if a particular train lets you roll your bike on without checking it as baggage, the timetable says that in the train's "Services" description.

To learn how to get the current Amtrak timetable, or for more information on Via Rail, see "Trains, national service" in Appendix B.

Amtrak's roll-on bike-storage racks on the Cascades line

BIKES ON

Before you go to the airport

See the table of pros and cons on page 197.

Find out how to ask on page 198.

Members of the League of American Bicyclists and the International Mountain Bicycling Association can ship their bikes separately at a discount. (To contact these organizations, see "National advocacy groups" in Appendix A).

If the airline gave you a separate receipt for their bike-transport fee, make sure you bring it with you when you check in.

Things to do

- ☐ Decide how you'll transport your bike
- ☐ Learn whether your airline supplies bike boxes
- ☐ If bike requires disassembly, practice at home
- ☐ Decide how to pack
- ☐ Pack a spare bike-lock key separate from the original
- ☐ Make sure you have tickets and other documentation
- ☐ If riding to or from an unfamiliar airport, get directions
- ☐ Figure how far in advance to leave for the airport

Think about packing two bags: One for stuff you want on the plane, such as book, maps, or food, and the tools you'll need to pack the bike (see page 202). Another bag for everything else.

Page 200 guides you.

STOP HERE AND READ

You can bring your bicycle onto an airplane like any other piece of luggage. But it's not simple. Airlines just aren't used to carrying bikes! Checking yours as luggage can cost lots, take much more time, and even make you miss your plane. But what if you like the freedom of riding into an airport, taking a flight, and riding out of your destination airport? These ideas will smooth the turbulence.

Item	Time required
Riding to the airport	Depends on distance
Getting a bike box	5 to 20 minutes
Packing a bike box	20 to 40 minutes
Checking in, if the agent freaks out	Up to 60 minutes
Long agent lines during airport rush hours	Up to 45 minutes

AIRPLANES

5 ways to fly your bike: pros and cons

Bike in no container whatsoever	Bike shop-supplied cardboard bike box	Airline cardboard bike box	Plastic bag or case	Collapsible bike
Don't have to get anything	Get before you travel	Get when arrive at the airport	Get before you travel	Get before you travel
Costs nothing	Usually can get for free each time you travel	Costs $5 to $20 (US)	Costs $75 to $400 (US) one time	Costs $400 to $2400 (US) one time
Lets you bike to the airport	Can't bike to the airport	Lets you bike to the airport	Can't bike to the airport	Lets you bike to the airport
No packing needed	Can pack before you go to airport	Must pack at the airport, adding time and hassle	Can pack before you go to airport	Must pack at the airport, but takes less time than an airline box
Nothing to keep or throw away	Throw away at your destination	Throw away at your destination	Travels with you like luggage	Travels with you like luggage
Airlines charge up to $200 (US) to transport a bike one way (some charge nothing)	Airlines charge up to $200 (US) to transport a bike one way (some charge nothing)	Airlines charge up to $200 (US) to transport a bike one way (some charge nothing)	If sum of 3 dimensions is less than a bike one way (usu. 62"), there's no charge	If sum of 3 dimensions is less than a certain length (usu. 62"), there's no charge
Bike can get bent, scratched, and dented	If packed right, protects your bike well	If packed right, protects your bike well	Protects your bike well	Protects your bike well
Airline might require a container	Always allowed	Always allowed	Always allowed	Always allowed

Smart Ideas

➤ Sometimes you can avoid the airline's bike-luggage fee by taking your bike right to a skycap at curbside. When you ask the skycap to check your bike, hold out a ten-dollar bill. But don't give it to him unless he agrees to check your bike.

➤ You might save trouble and cost if you simply rent a bike at your destination. To find and reserve rental bikes throughout the U.S. and Canada visit www.rentabikenow.com.

Getting an airline bike box

Two days before your flight, call the airline's main reservation number.

Say "I'm flying the day after tomorrow out of blah-blah-blah airport with my bicycle. Can you tell me whether they have bike boxes in stock?"

NO

Ask whether they can tell you if another airline in the same terminal offers boxes.

YES

Ask whether the ticket agent can give you the box or if you must go to a special baggage area. Ask whether they give away used boxes for free.

NO

Call the airline.

YES

Bike stores throw out lots of new-bike boxes. Check whether there's a bike shop close to the airport. Call and see if they'll let you come in and get a throw-away box.

Danger

If you use the connecting-flight scam to get a cheap airfare, don't bring your bike on the plane. Why? With the scam, you'd book a flight to somewhere you don't want to go, making sure the flight connects through your desired destination. Then you'd simply get off at your destination. You wouldn't get on the connecting flight—but your bike would!

Smart Idea
You might find that shipping your bike to a friend or bike shop at your destination comes out cheaper than taking it with you on a plane. (E.g., approximate UPS charges to ship a bike: Chicago to L.A. $130, Dallas to N.Y. $125.)

They give you an airport phone number

Call and say "I'm flying the day after tomorrow out of your airport with my bicycle. Do you have bike boxes in stock?"

YES

Ask whether they give away used boxes for free.

YES/NO

Ask whether the ticket agent can give you the box or if you must go to a baggage office.

Baggage office

Ask what hours the office is open.

NO

Ask whether they can tell you if another airline in the same terminal offers boxes.

NO

Bike stores throw out lots of new-bike boxes. Check whether there's a bike shop close to the airport.

Call and see if they'll let you come in and get a throw-away box.

YES

Call the airline.

Riding in and out of airports

STOP HERE AND READ

You can take public streets to many airports. But some airports let you arrive only by streets or highways that don't allow bikes. And local road maps often don't show all the ways in and out. Know what to look for.

Hotel shuttle vans:
An easy way to get in or out of the airport with your bike. Leaving the airport, pretend you're going to the hotel. Going to the airport, go to the hotel and pretend you've just checked out. Either way, the shuttle driver won't try to check your story.

Smart Idea
Two good sources of directions:
➤ Local bike advocates
See Appendix A for the local advocacy group. Call them and ask who might know about airport access.
➤ Car-rental agency maps
Call a major car-rental agency and ask for the phone number of their counter at the airport. Call the agency's counter and ask if they could send you a map.

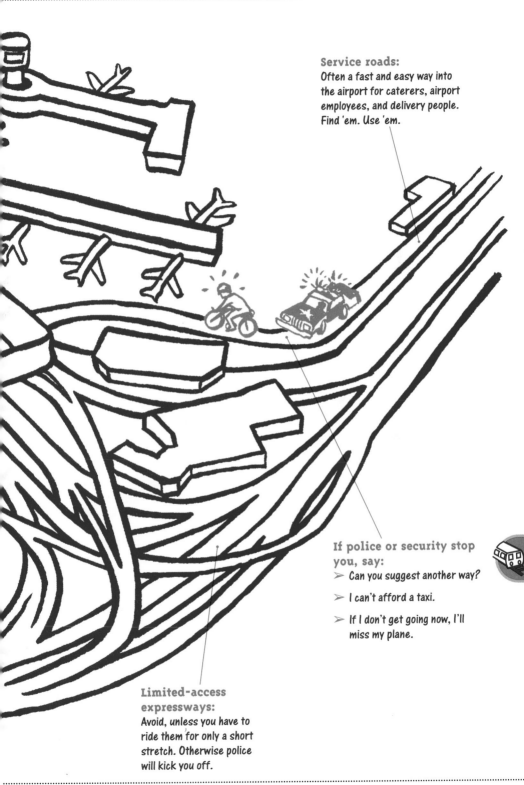

Service roads:
Often a fast and easy way into the airport for caterers, airport employees, and delivery people. Find 'em. Use 'em.

If police or security stop you, say:
➢ Can you suggest another way?

➢ I can't afford a taxi.

➢ If I don't get going now, I'll miss my plane.

Limited-access expressways:
Avoid, unless you have to ride them for only a short stretch. Otherwise police will kick you off.

Packing your bike into a box

W hen you fly your bike, you can pack your box in one of two kinds of cardboard bike boxes: (1) an airline box, for which you pay your airline; and (2) a smaller manufacturer's box, used to ship new bikes to stores. This page tells you how to pack a top-loaded airline box. (Pack side-loaded boxes almost the same way.) To learn how to pack a manufacturer's box, talk to a bike store employee. (You can get manufacturer's boxes from bike stores for free, because they discard the boxes.)

STOP HERE AND READ

WHAT YOU'LL NEED

Knife, box cutter, or scissors

Duct or filament tape, or 3"-wide plastic tape

Adjustable wrench

Wrenches that can loosen your handlebars and seat

Writing marker

1 If the bike has a water bottle, empty it into a nearby plant, fountain, or curb.

2 Unfold the box and stand it upright. Fold the end flaps in, and then the side flaps.

3 Tape over the top of the box at each side and the middle.

4 Turn the box over so the open end is on top. Lean it against a wall.

5 Using the adjustable wrench, remove the bike's pedals. As you face the right pedal, unscrew the pedal shaft counter-clockwise. As you face the left pedal, unscrew the pedal shaft clockwise.

6 Attach the pedals to the seat stay by wrapping them firmly with tape.

7 If you want to put a bag or pannier in the box, put it in the middle of the bike's frame. Attach it by wrapping firmly with tape or bungee cords.

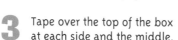
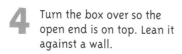
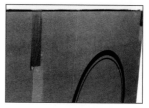

Airline box

Manufacturer's box

8 Remove the handlebars and lay them along the top tube.

9 Stand the box up next to the bike. Make sure the seat is low enough to fit into the box. If it isn't, lower or remove the seat. (If you remove it, tape it to the top tube.)

10 Attach a luggage tag (showing your name, address, and phone number) to the bike's frame and any bags going into the box.

11 Stand the box next to a wall and pull back the flaps.

12 Put the bike in front of the box. If the bike has a kickstand, raise it.

13 Grab the bike with one hand at the bottom of the seat post tube, and the other hand at the wheel and down tube. Lift the bike and lower it slowly into the box. (Side-loaded boxes: roll the bike into the box.)

14 Fold the end flaps in, and then the side flaps. Tape the top of the box in the middle.

15 Stand the box up on one end. Tape completely around one side and the middle so the flaps stay shut. (Side-loaded boxes: Leave the box sitting on its bottom and tape the box side to side, not top to bottom.)

16 Stand the box up on the other end. Tape completely around the other side.

17 Stand the box on its bottom. Tape completely around the middle.

18 With the marker, write your name, address, and phone number on each of the two faces of the box.

Checking in at the airport

When you approach an airline ticket counter and say you have a bike, some airline ticket agents know just what to do. But others freak out. Here are some ideas about how to handle them.

STOP HERE AND READ

How ticket agents might trip you up

Agent does this	Why it's a problem
Doesn't know how to charge you for a bike	Delays you
Can't find a bike box	Delays you
Makes you get the bike box from the baggage office	Delays you
Won't let you leave the counter to pack your bike	You don't have enough room to pack the box
Makes you check your bike separately at a baggage office	Delays you
Doesn't quickly get a baggage handler to take your packed bike box	Your bike might not get on your plane

Smart Idea

Before you get into a check-in line, put your bike where you can see it easily. One good place is right up against the ticket counter, at an unattended agent position.

What to do

- Arrive at the airport soon enough to allow for this.
- Don't offer to tell how much they should charge you, because they might charge you less.

If you've already verified that the airline has boxes, say so. If they still don't find one, insist that they get one from another airline.

- Arrive at the airport soon enough to allow for this.
- When you go to the baggage office, take your bike.

Point to an area within view of the counter, and tell the agent you'll be in plain sight.

Learn whether the baggage office can also check you in and assign your seat.

Unless it will make you miss your flight, hang around the ticket counter until a baggage handler takes your bike. If no one takes it within ten minutes, talk to a ticket agent.

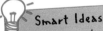

Smart Ideas

When you arrive at your destination:

- Where do you get your bike? In most airports, bikes come out separate from other baggage. Ask an airline employee where.
- To avoid having to get a new box on the return trip, ask whether the airline will save your box until you return to the airport. If they will, flatten the box and write your name on it.

Smart Idea

What if an airport employee won't let you bring your bike into a terminal or a ticket area, or tells you to move your bike while you're getting checked in? Don't flip out at them. Instead, you can help teach them that bicyclists have the same rights as any passenger with luggage: Gently but firmly say that an airline representative told you to be where you are. Tell them that your bike will be out of their way in just a few minutes.

BIKES IN CARS

WHAT YOU'LL NEED

➤ Bungee cord
➤ Medium or large sized rag

STOP HERE AND READ

To carry a bike with a car, most people think you must attach a bike-carrying rack to the car. Wrong! You can put almost any bike into just about any car without special equipment—just a bungee cord. And you can usually carry two bikes. This page shows how.

1 Open the car's trunk. Make sure you have at least one foot of space (from top to bottom) into which you can slide the bike.

2 Remove accessories such as bags and headlights from the bike.

3 Stand in front of the trunk with the bike on the opposite side of you. Have the bike's gears facing away from you.

4 Reach over the bike and with your right hand grab the bottom of the seat post tube. With your left hand grab the head tube.

5 Pick up the bike and slide it horizontally into the trunk. Leave the handlebars and front wheel outside the lip of the trunk. (To load another bike, slide it on top of the first bike, but slightly off to one side.)

6 Lower the trunk lid and see where on the bike's frame the lid hits the bicycle. Open the lid, then tie a rag around the frame where the lid will hit it (so nothing gets scratched).

7 Hook one end of a bungee cord into a hole on the underside of the trunk lid, and let the cord hang. (If you can't find a hole, hook the cord to the trunk lock.)

8 Lower the lid until it touches the bike's frame. (The handlebars and front wheel should stay outside of the trunk lid.) Then, holding the end of the bungee cord tightly, hook the bottom of the cord to the bottom of the car's bumper or to the underside of the car.

NIGHT & BAD WEATHER

Page 208

Afraid of the dark? You should be, if you bicycle at night without **lighting up your body and your bike**. Statistics say that cyclists with no lights or reflectors are the ones who get hit at night. So you're lots safer if you get bright. This chapter tells you how.

Getting bright doesn't have to cost a lot. What are the **cheap alternatives to reflective suits and fancy headlights**? Learn how to make your own in this chapter.

Page 212

The **smart night-riding ideas** don't stop with lights. Veteran night cyclists have a few tricks for how to ride. This chapter reveals them.

Page 213

The more you ride, you might wonder why cold weather should stop you. After all, plenty of northerners **bicycle in the fall and winter—and feel pretty warm** when they do. What do they know about the right ways to dress? This chapter tells you.

Page 214

Say you learn how to keep darkness and cold from thwarting your bike rides. Now what? Well, there are plenty of tricks that make it **easy to bike in rain and snow**. Some have to do with how you dress. Others involve little things you do to your bike. Still others concern how you ride. All are described in this chapter.

Page 218

Page 219

CHOOSING REFLECTIVE MATERIAL

When you buy a bike accessory that contains reflective material, what color material should you get? At night, reflective silver reflects several times brighter than either fluorescent orange, fluorescent yellow, or reflective white. But during the day, fluorescent pink, orange, or yellow makes you seen more easily. So if you can, get something colored bright pink, orange, or yellow with sections of reflective silver.

reflective white
standard brightness

fluorescent orange
(actual color not shown)
1.75 times standard brightness

reflective silver
5 times standard brightness

You can buy reflective material to put on your clothes by sewing, sticking, or ironing. Avoid the stick-on kind, because it often comes off after several washes. Get one of two kinds of reflective Scotchlite material: Reflective Transfer Film that you can press onto clothing with a clothes iron; or Reflective Fabric that you can sew on to light- or medium-weight fabrics and wash in warm water. To find the nearest Scotchlite distributor, contact 3M (listed under "Lighting" in Appendix B).

Also, picture how you look at night to motorists behind you. Reflective stuff on your clothes and bike should make it obvious you're a bicyclist. Smart ideas:

➤ Put reflective material on the sides, top, bottom, and sleeves of your jacket to make a reflective outline of your upper body.

➤ When headlights shine on you, keep pedaling. Motorists will see the up-and-down motion of your pedal's reflectors.

Equipment

Recommended Product
Reflective Yield Symbol
When headlights hit this reflective triangle, motorists can see it from 3,000 feet (915 meters). And it straps on over any clothes, so even a dark jacket has something bright. Have your bike dealer order from Jogalite, listed under "Lighting" in Appendix B. (For more on Mr. Bike's Recommended Products, go to www.mrbike.com/products.)

Rear light
Red strobe lights are most popular. Not needed if you have a good rear reflector.
If buying just one light, get a good headlight. Note that some places require a rear light at night.

Rear reflectors
Biggest are best. Get one at least three inches wide, and make sure it's pointed straight and not up or down. Many places require red, but amber is much brighter. Reflectors work only if they're clean, so remember to wipe them off! Required by law for night riding.

Smart Idea
If you put a rear carrying rack on your bike, move the back reflector to the end of the rack—so stuff you carry doesn't block it. If the reflector sticks up over the top of the rack, mount it with an extension.

NIGHT

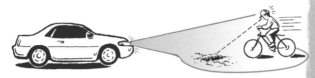

STOP HERE AND READ

Only three percent of bike rides take place at night— but over half of all cyclists killed get hit while riding at night without lights. Under bright street lights you need bike lights to be *seen*, not to see. But lights aren't enough. Because your upper body appears at eye level to most motorists, they'll see you easily if you wear bright stuff at night.

Smart Idea
The streetlights in some towns don't light up the pavement very well. But the headlights of oncoming cars can help. If you wear a cap or helmet with a visor, you can keep headlights out of your eyes so you can use the headlights to see the road.

Reflective orange safety vest
Good for cycling in dark clothes. Don't wear dark clothes, unless you add some light-colored material.

Clear glasses or goggles
Needed if airborne dirt bothers your eyes. Get wraparound glasses, so dirt can't enter from sides.

Jacket
Bright color, reflective piping in back.

Reflective tape
Use white facing front and red facing back. These colors help motorists see what direction you're going in.

Headlight
Required by law for night riding in most of North America. Battery-powered halogen or LED. Get the most powerful one you can afford. How to choose? See page 210. In a pinch, tie on a flashlight with rubber bands or a bungee cord. Generator lights can be bright, but many go dark when you stop.

Spoke reflectors
Put one on each wheel and keep them clean.

Reflective ankle strap

Tips for buying headlights

At night, the law in much of North America requires a white front light visible from 500 feet (150 meters). That's not much, considering you can see car headlights from 3,000 feet—and headlights are what most motorists look for. So it's smart to have a headlight almost as bright. This page tells you what to think about when choosing a headlight system.

STOP HERE AND READ

GENERATOR-POWERED LIGHT

WHY & WHY NOT

👍 No batteries

👍 Leave it on the bike

👍 Weighs less than batteries

👍 Newest models mount in wheel hub or bottom bracket (where the pedal arms connect), not by the tire. Have your dealer order from distributors listed under "Lighting" in Appendix B.

👎 Darkens when you stop (unless light can store power)

👎 Slows you down somewhat

New Words

Halogen
Halogen bulbs contain gas that make them brighter and last longer than incandescent, non-halogen bulbs.

LED
Light Emitting Diode: A type of bulb that uses less power longer than an incandescent bulb does. LEDs are brighter—and they stay brighter when batteries run low.

Lumen
A measure of how much a light illuminates the things on which it shines. Headlight makers sometimes rate their lights in lumens, or in similar units called "lux" or "candlepower."

How much do you want to spend?

How bright a light do you need?

How does the headlight mount?

Do you want to aim the headlight easily?

How long should the light last?

What does the charger cost?

Can you replace the battery?

Where does the battery go?

In what temperatures will you ride?

Do you like to build stuff?

If you can spend only $30 (US) or less, get a headlight with white LED bulbs (the more bulbs, the better). They have the best brightness and battery use for the price.

Brighter headlights usually cost more. For LED lights: To be seen as well as a car under bright streetlights, pay at least $300; to light your route in a dim setting, pay at least $70; to simply be seen at night, pay at least $20. To compare headlights, learn how bright the manufacturer rates them in terms of lumens, lux, or candlepower.

> A handlebar-mounted light should come with mounting hardware.
> Your handlebars should have room for the light. (If not, see the accessory bar shown on page 15.)
> Some lights mount near the wheel. But higher is better for you to be seen.
> If you leave your bike unattended, the light should be easy for you (or hard for a thief) to remove.

If you want a light you can quickly point in any direction —such as in a motorist's face—check out helmet-mounted lamps. Some come with hard-ware that lets them mount to almost any helmet.

> For how many hours do you need the light to work in a single day? The light's batteries should power the light at full strength for that period without recharging. (Unless, e.g., you bike to work in morning darkness, from work in evening darkness, and you can charge the batteries in between.) And if your night ride takes you away from streets and motorists: Look for headlights with both a high and low beam. (Away from traffic, use the low beam to make your battery last longer.)
> The newest battery-free, induction-powered lights (see p. 239) use mag-nets on the bike's wheel. They don't run out of power and last for years.

see p. 239

Some headlights come with their own chargers. If you consider one that doesn't, learn what kind of charger you need and its cost. And if you have other battery-operated devices, consider running them with rechargeable batteries—making a new charger more cost-effective.

Avoid headlights having their batteries sealed inside.
If a battery goes bad, you must replace the whole unit.

The batteries for some headlights go into a unit separate from the light itself. You should have a place (e.g., handlebar bag, carrying rack) in which to put them.

If you'll use the headlight at very cold temperatures, the light's battery should work in such cold. If it doesn't, learn whether a different type of battery will work.

If so, consider making your own headlight system—many people do.
See page 212 for more info.

A homemade headlight system

Headlight
55 watt halogen driving light
$15 US (for a pair)
or
2.4 watt LED scooter light
$40 US
From automotive stores

There are lots of different ways to build your own headlight system. But each has only five main pieces: bulb, battery, wire, switch, and charger. The biggest choices involve the brightness of the bulb and the size of the battery. This page shows an example of a homemade headlight system that's cheaper yet brighter than most systems made for bikes. It also shows some of the options you have for each piece.

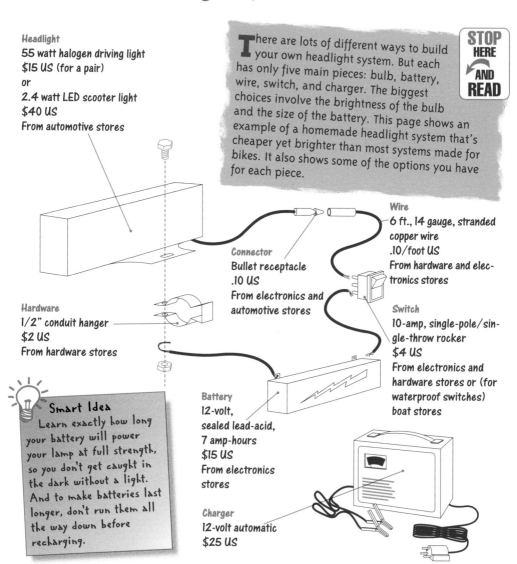

Wire
6 ft., 14 gauge, stranded copper wire
.10/foot US
From hardware and electronics stores

Connector
Bullet receptacle
.10 US
From electronics and automotive stores

Hardware
1/2" conduit hanger
$2 US
From hardware stores

Switch
10-amp, single-pole/single-throw rocker
$4 US
From electronics and hardware stores or (for waterproof switches) boat stores

Smart Idea
Learn exactly how long your battery will power your lamp at full strength, so you don't get caught in the dark without a light. And to make batteries last longer, don't run them all the way down before recharging.

Battery
12-volt,
sealed lead-acid,
7 amp-hours
$15 US
From electronics stores

Charger
12-volt automatic
$25 US

Bulb options

➤ 6- or 12-volt: More wattages available at 12.

➤ Halogen or non-halogen gas enclosure: Halogen brighter, lasts longer.

➤ LED: Compared to regular (incandescent) bulbs, runs longer on low batteries.

➤ 2 to 100 watts: Higher is brighter, but also hotter.

Rechargeable battery options

➤ 6- or 12-volt: Depends on bulb.

➤ Amp-hours: Battery charge = life amp-hours / [bulb wattage/volts]

➤ Lead-acid, NiCad, NiMH, Li-Ion, or alkaline: Most 6- & 12-volt batteries are lead-acid. Lead-acid holds a charge longer, then fades; Li-Ions, NiCads and NiMHs stay at almost max power till they quit. When not in use NiMHs lose charge more quickly than NiCads.

Charger options

➤ Lead-acid, NiCad, NiMH, or alkaline: Depends on battery.

➤ Manual or automatic: Automatic quits after battery is charged; manual can overcharge (and destroy) batteries.

On-street tips

Sometimes your headlights are not strong enough to make a motorist notice you. If you're stopped at an intersection in such a situation, signal the motorist by twitching your handlebars back and forth.

Until you're even with them, motorists coming from your sides often can't see your headlight. And their headlights won't hit your front or side reflectors. So assume they can't see you, and get ready to get out of their way.

Don't bike at night if your visual acuity's worse than 20/40 with glasses or contacts, or you can read a faraway sign or address OK in daylight but not at night. See a doctor to be sure.

If you're new at night riding, ride on streets where you already know the potholes and street layout. Riding on a familiar street makes it easier for you to learn about night riding. Also, if you're not sure about nighttime crime in a neighborhood, ask someone who knows, or don't ride alone.

Danger
If you're out after dark with no lights, pretend that no motorist can see you. When cars come from behind, get off the road and stop until they pass. When cars come from ahead or the sides, slow down and get ready to move out of their way.

Dressing for cold

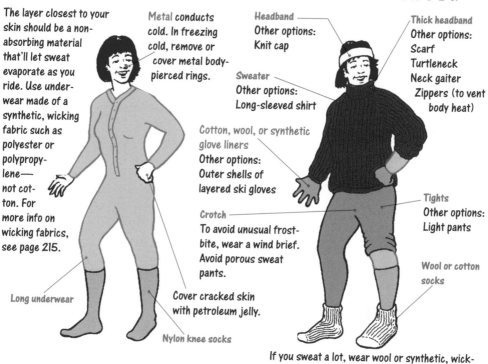

INNER LAYER

The layer closest to your skin should be a non-absorbing material that'll let sweat evaporate as you ride. Use underwear made of a synthetic, wicking fabric such as polyester or polypropylene—not cotton. For more info on wicking fabrics, see page 215.

Metal conducts cold. In freezing cold, remove or cover metal body-pierced rings.

Long underwear

Cotton, wool, or synthetic glove liners
Other options:
Outer shells of layered ski gloves

Crotch
To avoid unusual frost-bite, wear a wind brief. Avoid porous sweat pants.

Cover cracked skin with petroleum jelly.

Nylon knee socks

MIDDLE LAYER

Headband
Other options:
Knit cap

Sweater
Other options:
Long-sleeved shirt

Thick headband
Other options:
Scarf
Turtleneck
Neck gaiter
Zippers (to vent body heat)

Tights
Other options:
Light pants

Wool or cotton socks

If you sweat a lot, wear wool or synthetic, wicking fabrics for your middle layers. Cotton will trap the sweat.

STOP HERE AND READ

Cold weather cycling is a lot like snow skiing: You don't need a whole new set of clothes to bike in the cold. Instead, start with a sweat-shirt or jacket. In colder weather, add t-shirts, light sweaters, long underwear, and tights in layers. By wearing light layers you can remove outer clothes if you warm up while cycling. And when it's very cold, many cyclists don't need much insulation on their torsos and legs where heat builds up. But they do need extra insulation on their ears, hands, and feet, where blood circulates less.

You can fog-proof your glasses using juice from a raw potato. On each side of each lens, rub with a piece of the inside of a potato. Dry (but don't rub) with a lint-free cloth or paper towel.

If you have trouble breathing in freez-ing-cold or salt-satu-rated air, wrap a couple layers of scarves or bandannas around your mouth and nose.

SNOW

OUTER LAYER

Ski mask
Other options:
Balaclava

Ski goggles
Goggles that seal tightly against your skin are less likely to let your breath in and fog up. Also, don't use goggles that block your peripheral vision.

Earmuffs

Windbreaker

In freezing cold, having a thin inner glove helps when you have to use your fingers for things like locking. You can remove the outer glove.

Insulated mittens
Other options:
Gardening gloves
Fishing gloves
Thickly-lined hunters' gloves

Jeans
Wear black denim to hide road grime.
Other options:
Nylon overpants

Overlap clothes at the neck, wrists, waist, and ankles to seal out wind.

Shoes
Other options:
Boots
Rubber overshoes

Smart Idea
In cold weather, you might feel uncomfortably warm after riding for five to ten minutes. What if you don't want to stop and take off some clothing layers? Learn the minimum amount of clothes you need to feel comfortable after you've warmed up—then start out wearing only those clothes. You'll feel cold when you start, but you won't have to stop later.

FABRICS THAT WICK MOISTURE

Even in cold weather, you sweat when you bicycle. If sweat doesn't evaporate, it can build up inside your clothes and make you feel colder. You need two things to keep sweat from building up:

➤ Inner layers of clothes that wick sweat away from skin
➤ Outer layers that "breathe" or let moisture pass through to the outside air

How does a fabric wick sweat? It pulls sweat from inside the fabric and pushes the sweat outside. There, the moisture can evaporate in the air.

Synthetic, wicking materials go by many names. Here are some of them:

Acclimate
Bergeline
Capaline
Comfortrel
Coolmax
DriFit
Drylete
Filament polyester
Hydrofil
MerinoPerform
Polartec
Power Dry
Spun polyester
Thermastat
Thermax
Thermolite
Transpor
Vaporwick
Wick-lite

For suppliers of wet-weather clothing, see "Rain gear" in Appendix B.

Dressing for rain

New Words
Waterproof & Water-resistant
Rubber- or plastic-coated fabric is often water-proof: it doesn't let water in. But it doesn't let sweat out, which makes you clammy. Other fabrics are only water-resistant (or repellent): they stop wind, snow, and light rain, but will still get soaked in a downpour. Yet water-resistant fabrics are usually lighter, and dry out fast. Want to spend more? Get outerwear from materials that resist rain but let sweat out, such as Gore-Tex and Helly-Tech.

STOP HERE AND READ

For rain, you have options.
In hot weather: Don't dress for rain, just get wet. Carry dry clothes and a towel in a plastic bag.

For moderate temperature & short trips: Wear a poncho and gaiters, which get you a little wet but cut down sweat.

In cold weather: Wear a rain suit that keeps out all rain but makes you warm and maybe sweaty.

Before you put on your helmet, move the sides of the hood back so they don't block your peripheral vision.

Poncho
A waterproof poncho keeps rain off of your body, and lets air evaporate sweat from below. Sit on the back end so it doesn't fly around. Stick the front part under each hand.

Fog
Heavy fog gets you as wet as rain—so dress for it. If fog tends to show up unexpectedly where you ride, carry rain clothes.

Footwear
For extreme wet or snow, use rubber or waterproof overshoes such as those made by NEOS (listed under "Rain Gear" in Appendix B). To make shoes waterproof, use a sealer such as fabric cement, Aquaseal, Nikwax, Shoo Goo, Sno-Seal, or Welt Seal.

A plastic bag over each of your socks will keep your feet dry, and in cold weather keep them warm.

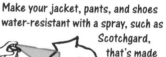
Make your jacket, pants, and shoes water-resistant with a spray, such as Scotchgard, that's made for this.

Jacket
Should have vents that let sweat evaporate. A hoodless jacket should have a high collar so water doesn't go down your neck.

Cyclist's rain cape
Similar to a poncho. But it has cords that loop around your thumbs and thighs to keep it in place. Order from Campmor (listed under "Rain gear" in Appendix B).

Pants
Black jeans or pants still look OK when wet or dirty.

Waterproof Rain Suit
Keeps rain out completely.

Equipping your bike

Grease

To keep water from rusting cables: Before you ride in rain or snow, cover the top end of each cable housing with a big gob of heavy-duty grease.

Brakes

Grime builds up on brake pads, making them squeak or scratch your rims. Run a rag between each pad and the rim, like shining a shoe. Occasionally remove the wheel and check the pads for wear.

Salt damage

With lots of winter riding, occasionally wipe your frame, rims, spokes, and derailleurs, and lube your chain (see page 32). Use a toothbrush for hard-to-reach parts.

Seat cover

Stuff a plastic grocery bag under your seat. When you park your bike outside in the rain or snow, put the bag over your seat. Later, you won't have to sit on a wet seat.

Rims

When wet, brakes grip aluminum rims better than they do steel.

Chain cover

Nylon shield protects your clothes when you lift or carry your bike. Helps keep dirt and salt off of your chain. Order from SRM Consulting (listed under "Rain gear" in Appendix B).

Carrying dry clothes

To keep clothes dry in panniers, backpack, or other carrying bags, coat the bags with a water-repelling spray. Or before you put your clothes inside the carrying bag, pack them in a plastic bag.

Bearings

After biking in wet weather, put your bike indoors so bearings can dry.

Tires

➤ If you ride a lot on wet pavement with slippery surfaces, use a deep-tread tire.

➤ If you ride a lot on ice, use a studded tire. Have your bike dealer order from All Weather Sports (listed under "Tires" in Appendix B).

➤ Another option: Use your current tires and follow the riding tips on page 219. (For a guide to tire treads, see page 23.)

Protective foot covers

Cut the fronts off of an old pair of boots and cut slits in the bottoms. Attach them to your pedals with reflective Velcro ankle straps.

Riding in snow

Too fast on hard pack
When riding too fast on hard-packed snow or ice, don't apply your front brake—you might skid out. Instead, turn into softer snow (that you might find on either side of a tire rut) to slow down.

Snow-narrowed street
With piles of snow on the right, ride in the middle of the right lane. If in light traffic motorists give you the horn, shake your head firmly and keep going. In heavy traffic, pull over and let cars pass.

Snow excuse
Snow's not an excuse to stay off your bike. Within a day of a major snowfall, snow crews usually clear most major streets. Walk your bike to one and get going.

Circulation
In extreme cold, wiggle your fingers often to keep blood circulating. If your toes freeze, get off your bike and run with it.

Don't suck exhaust
In cool or cold weather, notice when your face feels a blast of warm air. Most likely it's a blast from a car's exhaust. Hold your breath.

Hidden ice
Loose snow can hide ice on the pavement, so don't ride on it.

Parts freeze
In freezing weather, slush can freeze your derailleurs so you can't shift gears, freeze your brakes so you can't stop, and clog clip-in pedals. After riding through freezing slush:
➤ Before you park your bike outside, bounce the bike a couple of times. Also tap the derailleurs (and clip-in ped-als if you have 'em) with your foot. This shakes off slush.
➤ If you park your bike indoors, don't take it outside again unless it's dried off completely. If slush gets in your lock, spray inside it with WD-40 before taking it outside.

Riding in rain

Escape to transit

If your town allows bikes on buses or subways, bike on days when you normally wouldn't because rain threatens— then take transit if it does.

Bridges

When wet, bridges with metal-grated decks can you make wipe out if you have thin tires. Take the sidewalk or put both feet on the ground and push yourself across.

Slippery when wet

When it's wet outside, don't turn or brake suddenly on surfaces that get very slippery:

- Metal bridge grates
- Lane stripes
- Sewer and manhole covers
- Railroad tracks
- Leaves

Braking

When brake pads are wet, they take lots longer to work. Dry them by applying your brakes far ahead of where you want to slow down, causing your pads to wipe the rims. To dry them faster, pump the brakes by applying them, then letting go, over and over.

Can't brake

When you can't brake on a slick surface, put one pedal down (in the 6 o'clock position). Put the other foot on the ground, heel first, in front of the pedal and let your foot skid.

Riding over slick surfaces

Put your pedals at the 3 and 9 o'clock positions, and go loose at your elbows and knees. Ride straight until you get past the slippery area.

Start of rain

Don't race to beat the rain when it starts. That's when the streets are the most slick, because oil and antifreeze on the road spread before they wash away. The same thing happens in heavy fog. In these conditions, make turns more slowly so you don't wipe out.

Puddles

Don't ride through a puddle if you can't see the bottom. It could be a deep pothole that can make you crash or bend a rim.

Fender options

Fenders help keep you dry and clean. Why? In wet weather your front tire sprays dirty water on your feet and legs, and your rear tire sprays your back. The more of your tire a fender covers, the less spray you'll get on your body. Here are some options.

STOP HERE AND READ

CHEAP

Make a rear fender longer by cutting a triangular piece of rubber. Drill holes through the bottom of the fender and the top of the rubber piece. Bolt the rubber piece on. Put the heads of the bolts on the inside of the fender so they don't rub the tire.

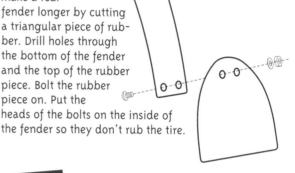

CHEAP

Cover a long strip of cardboard or wood with a plastic bag or plastic wrap. Bungee it to your rear carrying rack to keep your rear tire from spraying your back.

GOOD

If you buy fenders:

➤ Look for thick struts that won't bend.
➤ Fenders that hug the tires should be adjustable, in case they start to rub.
➤ If you use your bike year-round or carry it often in a vehicle, get easy-to-remove fenders.

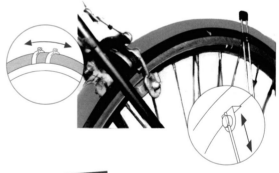

CHEAP

Cut a two-liter plastic bottle in half lengthwise and cut a pair of slits near both the top and bottom. Mount the plastic on the back of the **down tube** with the bottle's inside facing front. Tie it to the down tube by running tape, twist ties, or zip ties through the slits. Make sure it doesn't interfere with the derailleur cables.

RUDE

Short horizontal fenders can be very convenient: You can mount them easily and many are made to snap right off. They keep most of the spray off your back, but soak anybody who rides behind you.

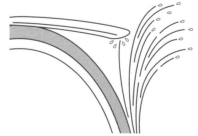

AVOIDING HAT HEAD & SWEAT

Does bicycling (or wearing a helmet) mess up your hair? Lots of people have the same problem. Folks with all kinds of hair—long, curly, 'fro, stringy—have secrets about **how to avoid helmet head, sweat head, or fly-away hair**. This chapter reveals these secrets.

Page 222

Maybe you've got other reasons for avoiding helmets. Like, you don't know death and injury statistics. Well, they're in this chapter. But, more important, it's easy to pay way too much for a helmet. Or get one that fits badly. You can **avoid bad fit and high cost** if you read this chapter.

Page 225

Enough about heads. What about the rest of your body? Maybe you've noticed people who bike to work all summer long. Many wear suits at their jobs. So they've got lots of **tips on how to control sweat**—few of which mean sweating less. Most of their tips involve changing clothes or toweling off. Find all of them in this chapter.

Page 228

By the way, **women have a few extra ideas about how to dress** for biking to work. Some have figured out how to wear skirts of every length. And what to do about some of the more gender-specific problems of hot-weather riding. This chapter tells all.

Page 232

HAIR

Dealing with helmets and wind

PROBLEM

Helmet crushes your hair.

SOLUTION 1

Wear a headband, bandanna, or scarf under your helmet.

SOLUTION 2

Get your hair permed. After removing your helmet, lightly fluff your hair with your fingertips.

How to turn a kerchief into a hair bandanna

Some people use their hair as an excuse: an excuse not to wear a helmet, or even an excuse not to ride their bike. If you're worried about bike hair or helmet head, check out these tips.

STOP HERE AND READ

Problem: Long hair gets whipped around by the wind.

Solution: Wear a bandanna, headband, or scarf.

Problem: Rain gets through your helmet vents and soaks your hair.

Solution: Buy a helmet cover, and wear plastic wrap or a plastic bag underneath it.

Problem: Your ponytail doesn't fit well under your helmet.

Solution: A helmet with either:
➤ A rear stabilizer (see p. 224) that has a large enough opening.
➤ No rear stabilizer, so your ponytail can hang down in back.

Aluminum or duct tape

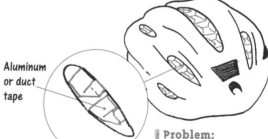

Solution: Make vent louvers that block light but let air in. Or apply sun block to your head.

Problem: You're bald, and you get tan stripes from your helmet vents.

Fixing your hair after a bike commute

Problem	Tactic
In humid weather, hair gets wild or frizzy	Before you ride, wash your hair with a shampoo made to remove oil from the scalp. Avoid tar-based shampoos, which can make your hair oilier. (See Smart Idea.)
Hair gets wet from sweat	Shampoo before you ride. At your destination, have a blow dryer and comb or brush handy.
Straight hair goes limp, curly hair gets frizzy	A heated styling comb can put a curl into the end of your straight hair, or straighten out wild hair.
	Apply hair spray before your ride. At your destination, fluff your hair with your fingertips. If needed, apply more spray.
In dry weather, hair curls up	Use a hair conditioner before cycling.
In hot weather, hair gets smelly	Apply perfumed oils to the foam pads on the inside of your helmet.
In hot weather, head gets too hot	Water squirted onto your hair will cool your head. If you wear a helmet, squirt into the vents.

Before I leave the house, I shower and dry my hair. When I get to work, my hair is soaked with sweat . But I keep hair-care stuff in my desk. I just blow-dry my hair and I look like a completely different person!

Carole Weiss
bicycles to work in Simi Valley CA

Smart Idea
Use a shampoo containing salicylic acid. Salicylic acid strips oil from the scalp, leaving your hair and scalp dry. When bicycling makes you sweat, the excess oil won't mess up your hair.

THREE BASIC HAIR STYLES

PONYTAIL

If you have long hair, a ponytail keeps your hair from getting whipped by the wind. In hot weather, a ponytail keeps your hair off your neck for coolness.

SHORT HAIR

A close cut stops wind, sweat, and helmets from messing up your hair.

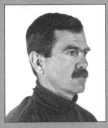

CUSTOM CUT

Put on your helmet or your usual cycling headwear, and take a long bike ride. Then bike to your hair stylist. Show them how your hair looks after cycling. Tell them to give you a haircut that will make your hair look good for biking.

HELMETS

Helmet features

Hard shell

Most helmets have a thin plastic surface. Avoid dark colors and flat finishes that make you less visible. Also avoid raised lumps or fasteners that might snag on something and cause you to break your neck.

Vents

The more vent space a helmet has, the cooler your head will stay in hot weather. If you're bald, see page 222 to learn how to avoid weird tan lines.

Rear stabilizer

(Not available on some helmets.) Presses on the back of your head. Keeps the helmet from moving in a crash—important, because in a crash your head might bounce. If you wear a ponytail, get a rear stabilizer that has room for a ponytail (see page 222).

Some helmets have stabilizers with a dial or sliding adjustor. You can make the helmet more snug by turning or sliding the adjustor.

Strap junctions

Should be adjustable so you can loosen or tighten the helmet after a haircut or when you wear stuff over your ears. **Best fit:** Adjust the junctions so that the straps come to a "V" directly under your ear.

Inside straps

Can give your helmet a very snug fit. On many helmets you can make the straps tighter or looser using a dial or slider on the rear stabilizer, described below.

Fitting Pads

Older helmets come with removable foam pads of different thicknesses. To get a tighter fit, insert thicker pads. For a looser fit, use thinner pads or remove the pads.

Chin Buckle

Usually one buckle connects to all the straps. Some helmets have a thin rubber ring that keeps the strap from slipping. If your helmet doesn't have one, put a small rubber band on the strap. **Best fit:** You have the buckle tight enough so when you open your mouth wide, you feel the helmet press down on your head.

Smart Idea
If you ride at night, put reflective tape (see page 209) or a reflective elastic band on your helmet. Remember that your head's the highest part of your body: If your helmet reflects headlights, motorists will see you better.

Soft shell

How a hard-shell helmet looks without the shell. Often comes with a cloth helmet cover, which you can buy separately (avoid dark colors). **Danger:** Soft shells are less smooth than hard, and easily get holes and bumps—so if one slides during a fall, your head could snag on something.

Visor

Only needed if you often ride into sunrise or sunset, or into headlights on dark streets (see page 209). The visor should attach with Velcro or snap-out tabs—so when the helmet crashes, it falls off easily. Otherwise, it could get snagged on something and cause you to break your neck.

> **Smart Idea**
> Instead of paying extra for a visored helmet, wear a baseball cap or cheap sun visor under your helmet. Or make one yourself with a piece of rigid plastic and stick-on Velcro strips.

Aerodynamic design

The rounder and smoother a helmet is, the more it'll protect you. But it won't help you go faster—no matter how aerodynamic it looks—unless you're moving at warp speed.

STOP HERE AND READ

Every year in the U.S., almost a thousand cyclists die or suffer brain damage from head injuries. Most of these injuries can be prevented by wearing helmets. What's most important in a helmet? Two things: a good fit and wearing the helmet properly.

HOW HELMETS WORK

When you crash, an abrupt stop can crack your skull and bruise your brain. That won't usually happen when you wear a helmet, because helmets make your head stop more gradually. A helmet "absorbs" the energy of the crash.

WHEN TO REPLACE A HELMET

Replace your helmet if you ever crash it. Even if it looks OK, its innards will be so screwed up that it won't protect you again. Otherwise, there isn't much evidence that a five- or ten-year-old helmet won't still protect you—even though some manufacturers say helmets "degrade" after only a few years. So if you haven't crashed a helmet, good reasons to replace it are to:

➢ Get a better fit because of new fastening systems.

➢ Get more protection because of new technology or revised standards.

For the latest helmet developments, contact the Bicycle Helmet Safety Institute (listed under "National advocacy groups" in Appendix A).

Sizing

Sizes

Some manufacturers make only two adult sizes. And some cheaper helmets come only in a single adult size. If you choose a brand that offers more sizes, chances are better you'll get a good fit. And if your head is larger than most, look for an XL size. (You can also find XXLs if you look around.)

How to find your size

➤ Put the helmet on your head.

➤ If the helmet seems to sit too high off of your head, or it won't cover half your forehead when it sits level, try a larger size.

➤ If you see a gap between the helmet's rim and your head, try adjusting the rear stabilizer if it has one. If you can't get a snug fit, try a smaller size.

➤ If a smaller size seems too small, take the larger size and either adjust it using the rear stabilizer or insert the thicker foam pads that come with the helmet.

Space

You should have as little space as possible between your head and the inside of the helmet—so that when you crash, your skull doesn't bang up against the helmet.

Danger
If your helmet doesn't fit right, it won't stay in one place when it crashes—so it might not protect your head.

How to put on a helmet in 3 steps

1 **Eyes:** When you look up you should see the helmet's front rim (not just the visor, if it has one). If you can't see the rim, tilt the helmet forward until you can. The front of the helmet should cover your forehead.

2 **Ears:** Snap the chin buckle closed. On each side of your head, the helmet's two straps should meet under your ear to form a V. If they don't, move the straps up or down through the junction.

3 **Mouth:** With the chin buckle closed, open your mouth wide. You should feel the helmet push down on your head. If it doesn't, take the helmet off and make the chin buckle's strap shorter by sliding the strap through the buckle.

Danger
Don't wear your helmet tilted back. It won't protect your skull if you crash on your forehead.

Cost

➢ You can get a good helmet for $20, even less if you look around.

➢ More costly helmets usually aren't much safer. But they have better ventilation, weigh less, and look sharp.

➢ Cheaper helmets usually aren't much heavier than expensive ones. Most cyclists notice no difference. If you think you need an ultra-light helmet, test-ride a regular one to make sure.

➢ You can pay lots for style. But even a low-cost helmet can look cool if you decorate it.

➢ Get a helmet with a replacement discount: If you crash the helmet, its manufacturer replaces it with 50 percent (or more) off the price.

Kids' helmets

Fit your kids' helmets the same way that you fit your own. And how do you make sure your kids wear their helmets? Set an example: Always wear yours!

CERTIFICATION

Look at the inside of a helmet, or the box it comes in, for safety certification. *Don't* buy a helmet unless it has one of these certifications.

> THIS HELMET COMPLIES WITH U.S. CPSC SAFETY STANDARD FOR BICYCLE HELMETS FOR PERSONS AGE 5 AND OLDER.

US Consumer Product Safety Commission

Snell B-90A

ASTM F1447
(actual size & shape may vary)

CSA D 113.2
ASTM F 1447

CSA DI13.2

Snell B-95A

Snell N-94
(actual color: yellow)

ANSI Z90.4 1984
(out of date)

HANDLING

How to pack wrinkle-free

Rolling

Fold where creases are least noticeable

Back side   Back side

Roll from top to bottom

Put belts & ties in shoes to save space

Pack shoes with bottoms together

Loose folding

Lay garments with ends sticking out

1

2

Starting at bottom, fold each garment in

3

Makes wide, crease-free folds

4

> **Smart Idea**
> If you take your clothes to work each day, keep spare clothes (especially socks, underwear, and shoes) at work—in case, one day, you forget to bring them.

Clothes at work

➤ On the weekend or start of the week, take five days' worth of clothes to work.
➤ At week's end, take your clothes to the cleaners.
➤ Pick up your cleaning from work and leave it at work.

CLOTHES & SWEAT

Dressing for the ride

In warm weather:

➤ Wear loose t-shirts, tank-tops, and shorts for good ventilation.

➤ If sweat gets in your eyes or face, wear a headband.

In cold weather, wear loose cycling clothes, your work clothes, and windbreaker in layers (see page 214) that you can remove in layers as you heat up.

Bags for carrying clothes

SIMPLE BACKPACK

WHY & WHY NOT

 Low cost

 Can bungee to your bike's rear rack

 Makes your back sweat

 Can't pack lots of extra stuff

HANDY PANNIERS

WHY & WHY NOT

 Can fit lots of stuff

 Attaches easily to your bike's rear rack

DELUXE BIKE GARMENT BAG

WHY & WHY NOT

 Don't have to fold stuff

 High cost for limited use

STOP HERE AND READ

In a coast-to-coast survey conducted for this book, over 85 percent of people who bike to work or school said they don't shower at their destinations. Do they just smell bad? No. Most erase bad odor by simply toweling off and changing into fresh clothes. If they want to feel even cleaner, they sponge off and apply talcum powder. As for clothes themselves: When weather's mild, they bike in the clothes they wear at work. On days when they'll sweat, they change clothes when they get to work.

Riding to work

To cut down on sweat, leave earlier and cycle more slowly.

If your route involves hills, find the roads with the most gradual inclines (see page 172).

Smart Idea
If you commute into the sun at dawn or sunset, wear a red or deep orange top. Don't wear white, because sun-blinded motorists behind won't see you.

Cleaning up at work

1 Change clothes and clean up in a washroom. For privacy, use a toilet stall.
➤ Use wheelchair-accessible stalls for the most room.

2 Remove your work clothes from your bag and hang them up.
➤ If stalls don't have wall hooks, buy adhesive ones and put them in the stalls yourself.

3 Take off your cycling clothes and put them in your bag.
➤ If you've nowhere to let cycling clothes dry, put them inside a plastic bag.
➤ If you store your bike in a secure, private area, lay your cycling clothes on the top tube and handlebars to dry.

4 Use a towel to dry off sweat.

5 If you feel smelly:
➤ Carry a package of disposable, moist towelettes and use them to sponge off. Or use a washcloth.
➤ Apply talcum powder.

6 Towel off hair, wet it if necessary, and brush, comb, and/or blow-dry (see page 223).

7 Put on jewelry away from toilets and sinks so you don't drop it in.

Work clothes to bike in

💡 Smart Idea
Some bike-grease stains won't come out in the wash. For tough grease stains, apply a degreasing hand soap (usually a waterless gel or cream) found in automobile-supply stores. (First check how it affects the fabric's color.)

Sunglasses or goggles
Keeps airborne debris out of your eyes. (For custom goggles, see "Can't find it?" on page 237.)

Key holder or chain
When you bike in clothes without pockets.

Kerchief
Comes in handy to wipe grime from bike contact or sweat from exertion.

Slacks
➢ Black or dark-colored pants don't show grime from your bike.
➢ If you often bicycle in the same pair of pants, the pants' seat can get shiny or faded—especially if they're corduroy or wool. Wear loose shorts over the pants.

Ankle strap
Keeps pants cuff from getting in chain or front gears.

Blazer or sports coat
On cool days, wear instead of windbreaker.

Bra
Large-breasted women find more comfort in athletic support bras.

Shirt or blouse
Loose enough to let air in.

Underwear
Nylon or other synthetics absorb sweat less than cotton.

Cuff tucked in socks
Keeps pants cuff from getting in chain or front gears.

Shoes
Soles have tread to grip pedals.

Skirts and dresses

A good cycling skirt:

➢ Isn't too tight to let you open your legs enough to pedal.

➢ Comes down no farther than the knees.

➢ Won't get caught in the back brakes.

➢ If it's shorter or wider than modesty allows, wear cycling shorts underneath.

➢ Try a "skort": a pair of shorts that look like a skirt.

Long dresses or skirts

1 Wear a belt.

2 Pull one or two feet of material up until the dress hangs at knee height.

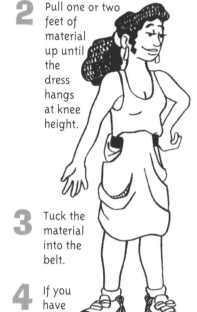

3 Tuck the material into the belt.

4 If you have no belt, tuck the dress into the waistband of your underwear.

Mounting a standard-frame bike in a skirt

1 Lay the bike on the ground.

2 Put one foot inside the middle of the frame.

3 Pull the bike up halfway.

4 Pull your foot out of the frame.

5 Stand the bike all the way up.

6 To get off the bike, reverse the steps.

It's hard to find a work skirt I can cycle in. Women's skirts often aren't flared enough. So I've bought skirts made for teenagers, which work fine.

Sue McNamara
bikes to work in Philadelphia

APPENDIX A
RESOURCE GUIDE

Contents

National advocacy groups

Alliance for Biking and Walking
PO Box 65150
Washington DC 20035
202/449-9692
info@peoplepoweredmovement.org
www.peoplepoweredmovement.org

Bicycle Helmet Safety Institute
4611 7th St. South
Arlington VA 22204
703/486-0100
info@helmets.org
www.helmets.org

Canadian Cycling Association
2197 Riverside Drive, Suite 203
Ottawa Ontario K1H 7X3
613/248-1353
general@canadian-cycling.com
www.canadian-cycling.com

International Mountain Bicycling Association
PO Box 7578
Boulder CO 80306
303/545-9011
info@imba.com
www.imba.com

League of American Bicyclists
1612 K St. NW, Suite 800
Washington DC 20006
202/822-1333
bikeleague@bikeleague.org
www.bikeleague.org

Rails-to-Trails Conservancy
2121 Ward Court NW, Floor 5
Washington DC 20037
202/331-9696
railtrails@transact.org
www.railstotrails.org

Local advocacy groups

If a U.S. town's not listed below, you can learn about its local bike-advocacy group from the League of American Bicyclists. The league is listed on page 233 in "National advocacy groups." Members can get the league's annual almanac that shows bicycling resources for every U.S. state.

Arizona
Atlanta Bicycle Coalition
PO Box 54488, Phoenix AZ 85078
602/686-1302
www.cazbike.com

Atlanta area
Atlanta Bicycle Campaign
233 Mitchell St., Suite 315
Atlanta GA 30303
404/881-1112
www.atlantabike.org

Baltimore and Maryland
One Less Car
1209 N. Calvert St., Baltimore MD 21202
410/960-6493
http://onelesscar.org

Boston and Massachusetts
Massachusetts Bicycle Coalition
171 Milk St., Suite 33, Boston MA 02109
617/542-2453
www.massbike.org

Chicago area
Active Transportation Alliance
9 W. Hubbard St., Suite 402
Chicago IL 60654
312/427-3325
www.activetrans.org

Connecticut
Bike Walk Connecticut
PO Box 270149, West Hartford CT 06127
860/521-8408
http://bikewalkconnecticut.org

Denver
BikeDenver
1536 Wynkoop St., Denver CO 80202
303/249-8621
http://bikedenver.org

Florida
Florida Bicycle Association
PO Box 718, Waldo FL 32694
352/468-3430
www.floridabicycle.org

Houston
BikeHouston
1302 Waugh, PMB #682, Houston TX 77019
713/222-2453
www.bikehouston.org

Indiana
Indiana Bicycle Coalition
201 S. Capital Ave., #800
Indianapolis IN 46225
317/466-9701
www.bicycleindiana.org

Los Angeles
Los Angeles County Bicycle Coalition
634 S. Spring St., #821, Los Angeles CA 90014
213/629-2142
www.la-bike.org

Maine
Bicycle Coalition of Maine
PO Box 5275, Augusta ME 04332
207/623-4511
www.bikemaine.org

Michigan
League of Michigan Bicyclists
416 S. Cedar St., Suite A, Lansing MI 48912
517/334-9100
www.lmb.org

Minnesota
Bicycle Alliance of Minnesota
PO Box 65766, St. Paul MN 55165
651/387-2445
www.bikemn.org

Mississippi
Bike Walk Mississippi
PO Box 2032, Oxford MS 38655
601/801-0176
www.bikewalkmississippi.org

Montreal and Quebec
Velo Quebec
1251 Rachel Street East
Montreal Quebec H2J 2J9
514/521-8356
www.velo.qc.ca

New York City
Transportation Alternatives
127 W. 26th St., #1002, New York NY 10001
212/629-8080
www.transalt.org

Oakland area
East Bay Bicycle Coalition
PO Box 1736, Oakland CA 94604
510/533-7433
www.ebbc.org

Philadelphia area
**Bicycle Coalition of
Greater Philadelphia**
1500 Walnut St., #1107, Philadelphia PA 19107
215/220-3004
www.bicyclecoalition.org

Portland and Oregon
Bicycle Transportation Alliance
PO Box 28289, Portland OR 97228
503/226-0676
www.bta4bikes.org

San Diego area
San Diego County Bicycle Coalition
PO Box 34544, San Diego CA 92163
858/487-6063
www.sdcbc.org

San Francisco
San Francisco Bicycle Coalition
833 Market St., Floor 10
San Francisco CA 94103
415/431-2453
www.sfbike.org

Seattle and Washington state
Bicycle Alliance of Washington
PO Box 2904, Seattle WA 98111
206/224-9252
http://bicyclealliance.org

Texas
Texas Bicycle Coalition
P.O. Box 1121, Austin TX 78767
512/476-7433
www.biketexas.org

Toronto
**Toronto Coalition for Active
Transportation**
5 Elizabeth St., Toronto Ontario M5G 1P4
416/392-0290
www.torontocat.ca

Washington, DC
Washington Area Bicyclist Association
2599 Ontario Rd. NW
Washington DC 20009
202/518-0524
www.waba.org

Vancouver (British Columbia) area
Vancouver Area Cycling Coalition
Box 47068, RPO City Square
Vancouver BC V52 4L6
604/878-8222
www.vacc.bc.ca

Wisconsin
Bicycle Federation of Wisconsin
PO Box 1224, Madison WI 53701
608/251-4456
www.bfw.org

World Wide Web sites

www.bicyclinginfo.org
Lots of background info and data for those who want to advocate for bicycling improvements in their communities.

www.bikemap.com
Steve Spindler's maps and access info for public-transit systems in major U.S. cities.

www.bikewinter.org
Winter bicycling events and tips.

http://draco.acs.uci.edu/rbfaq
An archive of rec.bicycles, useful on-line contributions of bikers from all over.

www.girlbike.com
How-to tips, product reviews and deals, and resources for female bike riders.

www.helmets.org
Bicycle Helmet Safety Institute reviews the latest products, debunks safety myths, more.

www.mapsonus.com,
www.ridethecity.com,
http://maps.google.com/biking
Each site creates an on-map route for a start and end you specify. Options include avoiding things along the way, safest vs. most direct route, and miles vs. kilometers.

www.mrbike.com
Mr. Bike's tips on many bike subjects, info for news media, and more about this book.

www.nordicgroup.us/fold
Huge resource about folding bikes.

www.icebike.org
Tips on bicycling in ice and snow.

www.wordspacepress.com
Learn how to get adult and child bike-safety publications customized for your area.

Bicycle touring

Adventure Cycling Association
PO Box 8308, Missoula MT 59807
800/755-2453
www.adventurecycling.org

Bike maintenance books

You can find many books that show you how to fix and maintain your bike. Here are a few we recommend.

Anybody's Bike Book,
by Tom Cuthbertson

The Bicycling Complete Guide to Bicycle Maintenance & Repair, by Todd Downs

Big Blue Book of Bicycle Repair,
by C. Calvin Jones

Simple Bicycle Repair,
by Rob Van der Plas

Bike safety booklets

Mr. Bike's *Bicyclist Survival* gives you all the bike safety information you'll need!

➢ Fully illustrated on 32 pages.
➢ Covers traffic basics, bike fit, off-road riding, and more.
➢ Perfect as a give-away at bike shops, bicycling events, and libraries, or as a text for biking classes.

How to order: Use the order form on the last page or at www.wordspacepress.com.

APPENDIX B
SUPPLIER DIRECTORY

Contents

Can't find it?

Do you need special clothes or equipment, and can't find them in any store? Maybe we can help. Mr. Bike has a big file of unique and custom-made products that wouldn't fit into this book. If you want help getting a hard-to-find product, check www.mrbike.com/products or contact Mr. Bike:

Mr. Bike

2445 North Artesian Avenue
Chicago IL 60647
773/292-0932 (voice and fax)
mrbike@mrbike.com

BICYCLE DEALERS:
You can use your own computer to find distributors for over 200,000 bicycling products—with a subscription to the Bike-alog on-line database. Bike-alog's database also provides bike specs, an automatic spoke-length calculator, and more. Call Bike-alog today at 800/962-1950 or e-mail to datacollection@bikealog.com.

Bells, whistles, & gadgets

All Weather Safety Whistle
PO Box 8615, St. Louis MO 63127
314/436-3332
www.stormwhistles.com
Have your bike dealer order:
Storm whistle, page 77.

Kauffman Marketing
PO Box 16846, Portland OR 97216
866/463-1314
www.greenlightstuff.com
Order direct:
Green Light Trigger, page 108.

Kool-Stop International
1061 S. Cypress St., La Habra CA 90632
800/586-3332
www.koolstop.com
Have your bike dealer order:
Kool-Stop "China Bell," page 76.

Bicycles, folding (page 4)

If your bicycle dealer doesn't carry folding bikes, ask them to learn about the models of folding bicycles available from the following bicycle companies.

Advanced Sports International
(Breezer), Philadelphia PA
Dahon California, Duarte CA
Giant Bicycle, Newberry Park CA
KHS, Rancho Dominguez CA
Trek Bicycle, Waterloo WI

Contact the following bicycle companies directly, to order or to find dealers.

Bike Friday
3364 W 11th Av., Eugene OR 97402
800/777-0258
www.bikefriday.com

Kinn-Ovations
5296 Greenleaf Dr., Swartz Creek MI 48473
810/232-2994
www.kinn-ovations.com

Montague
PO Box 381118, Cambridge MA 02238
800/736-5348
www.montagueco.com

Alex Moulton Bicycles
44 (0)1225 865895 (United Kingdom)
www.alexmoulton.co.uk

Peregrine Bicycle Works
11 Commerce Ct., #7, Chico CA 95928
877/729-2453
www.pbwbikes.com

Riese & Muller (Birdy)
49 (0)6151 366 86 0 (Germany)
www.en.r-m.de

Sling Shot Bicycle
342 Market St. SW, Grand Rapids MI 49503
888/530-5556
www.slingshotbikes.com

Swift Folders
280 Nevins St., New York NY 11217
718/875-3090
www.swiftfolders.com

C.M. Wasson Company (Brompton)
423 Chaucer St., Palo Alto CA 94301
800/783-3447
www.foldabikes.com

Bicycles, rental (page 197)

Rent a Bike Now
847/441-4292
www.rentabikenow.com

Bicycles, women's (page 4)

If your bicycle dealer doesn't carry bikes made especially for women, ask them to learn about the models of women's bicycles available from the following companies.

Bianchi USA
Cannondale
Diamondback
Felt
Fuji
Giant Bicycle
GT Bicycles
Joannou Cycle (Jamis)
Marin Bikes
Raleigh America
Schwinn Bicycle
Specialized
Terry Precision Cycling
Trek Bicycle

Bungee cords (page 16)

RiderWearHouse
8 S. 18th Av. West, Duluth MN 55806
800/222-1994
www.aerostitch.com
Order direct:
adjustable and multiple-strap bungees.

Handlebar parts

J&B Importers
11925 SW 128 St., Miami FL 33186
800/666-5000
www.jbimporters.com
Have your bike dealer order:
Pyramid stem riser, page 10.

TerraCycle
3450 SE Alder St., Portland OR 97214
800/371-5871
www.terracycle.com
Order direct:
Multi-purpose accessories mount, page 15.

Hardware

McMaster-Carr Supply
Atlanta GA 404/346-7000
Cleveland OH 330/995-5500
Elmhurst IL 630/833-0300
Los Angeles CA 562/692-5911
New Brunswick NJ 609/259-8900
www.mcmaster.com
Order direct: S-hooks, page 189.
Or visit your local hardware store.

Lighting

J&B Importers
11925 SW 128 St., Miami FL 33186
800/666-5000
www.jbimporters.com
Have your bike dealer order:
Shimano wheel-hub generators, page 210.

Yellow Jersey
419 State St., Madison WI 53703
608/257-4737
www.yellowjersey.org
Order direct:
Union bottom-bracket generators, page 210.

Jogalite
PO Box 149, Silver Lake NH 03875
800/258-8974
www.teamestrogen.com/co-b10015.html
Order direct:
reflective safety triangle, page 208.

Peter White Cycles
24 Hall Rd., Hillsborough NH 03244
603/478-0900
www.peterwhitecycles.com
Have your bike dealer order:
wheel-hub generators, page 210.

Reelight ApS
Hasselager Centervej 11, 1, 8260 Viby J, Denmark
45 8674 2490
www.reelight.com
Order direct:
battery-free, magnet-powered lights,
page 211.

3M Scotchlite Reflective Material
3M Center, St. Paul MN 55144
800/328-7098 (select #2)
www.3m.com/scotchlite
Call for nearest Scotchlite dealer (page 208).

Wilson Bicycle Sales
31157 Wiegman Rd., Hayward CA 94544
800/877-0077
Have your bike dealer order:
bottom-bracket generators, page 210.

Locks & accessories

ABUS
23910 N. 19th Av., Phoenix AZ 85027
800/352-2287
www.abus.com
Have your bike dealer order:
Granit X-Plus locks, page 54.

Kabletek Manufacturing
320 W. Lone Cactus Dr., #3, Phoenix AZ 85027
800/553-2453
www.kabletek-flexweave.com
Have your bike dealer order:
Flexweave cables, page 59.

Joannou Cycle
151 Ludlow Av., Northvale NJ 07647
800/222-0570
www.jamisbikes.com
Have your bike dealer order:
Bad Bones lock straps, page 51.

Kryptonite
437 Turnpike St., Canton MA 02021
800/729-5625
www.kryptonitelock.com
Have your bike dealer order:
bicycle locks, pages 54, 57.

Master Lock
137 W. Forest Hill Av., Oak Creek WI 53154
800/558-5528
www.masterlockbike.com
Have your bike dealer order:
bicycle locks, page 55.

St. Pierre Manufacturing
317 E. Mountain St., Worcester MA 01606
800/926-2342
www.stpierreusa.com
Have your bike dealer order:
QuadraChain, page 57.

Stocks Manufacturing
22 Robinson Road
Waterford Ontario N0E 1Y0
519/443-8475
www.stocksmfg.on.ca
Have your bike dealer order:
Stocks Lock, page 54.

Todson
73 N. Washington St.
North Attleboro MA 02760
800/213-4561
www.onguardlock.com
Have your bike dealer order:
OnGuard locks, pages 54-55, 57.

Winner International
32 W. State Street, Sharon, PA 16146
800/527-3345
www.winner-intl.com
Have your bike dealer order:
Ultra Bike Club Junior, page 55.

Pepper spray (page 136)

Defense Devices
111 S. Highland St., #144, Memphis TN 38111
901/268-5566
www.defensedevices.com
Order direct:
Police Magnum pepper spray.

Rain gear

Campmor
PO Box 700, Saddle River NJ 07458
800/226-7667
www.campmor.com
Order direct:
bicycle rain cape, page 216.

Gempler's
PO Box 44993, Madison WI 53744
800/332-6744
www.gemplers.com
Order direct:
NEOS overshoes, page 216.

SRM Consulting
2835 Aegean Pl., Castro Valley CA 94546
510/889-9752
www.wcfanshop.com
Order direct:
chain cover, page 217.

Registries, national (page 40)

Cycle Finders
3057 Cornelia Drive
Jacksonville FL 32257
787/422-2708
www.bikefinder.com

National Bike Registry
1475 Powell St., Suite 101
Emeryville CA 94608
800/848-2453
www.nationalbikeregistry.com

Tires

All Weather Sports
1540 Hayes Ave., Fairbanks AK 99709
907/474-8184
www.allweathersports.com
Order direct:
studded tires (page 217).

Nu-Teck
2751 W. Oxford Av., #1, Englewood CO 80110
800/290-8828
www.nu-teck.com
Have your bike dealer order:
airless tires (page 23).

Quality Bicycle Products
6400 W. 105th St., Bloomington MN 55438
800/346-0004
www.qbp.com
Have your bike dealer order:
studded tires (page 217).

Schwalbe North America
105-536 Herald St., Victoria BC V8W 1S6
888/700-5860
www.schwalbetires.com
Have your bike dealer order:
studded tires (page 217).

Trains, national service (page 195)

Amtrak (U.S.)
www.amtrak.com
To get the current Amtrak timetable, in the
U.S. call 800/872-7245 and press 3
for reservations.

Via Rail (Canada)
www.viarail.com
For information on fares and service, in
Canada call 888/842-7245.

Acknowledgments

Advisors & contributors

Mr. Bike would like to recognize the following individuals for their advice and participation.

Todd Allen
Maria Barnes
Vance Blume
Anji Brown
Frank Cesaro
George Christensen
John Ciccarelli
Mary Edsey
Ellen Fletcher
Bob Flor
John Forester
Justyna Frank
Ben Gomberg
Joan Gordon
Dean Gustafson

Bill Hoffman
Jenny Holan
Barbara Hughett
Steve Jajkowski
Derrick James
John Kaehny
Nancy Kendrew
Charlie Komanoff
Charles Kurre
Kevin & Sandy Lamm
Bill Lang
Bonnie McClun
Keith Mistrik
Dru Moorhouse

Anita Nebel
Tom Northfell
Ed Ravin
Rich Ries
Misty Romero
Gail Smith
Dave Snyder
Chris Stodder
Ann Sullivan
Randy Swart
David Takemoto-Weertz
Gale Wallencamp
Barb Wentworth
Chris West

Mr. Bike also thanks the hundreds of people whose tips appear in this book.

Photo contributors

ABUS Lock
Aero Design & Manufacturing
All-Weather Safety Whistle
Avocet
Bell Sports
Bike Nashbar
Bike Track
Buckley/Friedman
Bykaboose International
Canadian Standards
    Association
C.H. Hanson Company
Dahon California
Delta Cycle
Go Boulder
GT Bicycles

ISM Saddles
Karl Haas
Jim Hamre
Hobson Associates
Patty Howells
Kabletek Manufacturing
Kryptonite
Master Lock
Cynthia McArthur
Sue McNamara
Karen Frost Mecey
Metro Transit (Seattle)
Mary Ellen Paquette
Planet Bike
Carolyn Prieb
Sidetrak

Snell Memorial Foundation
Speed Defies Gravity
Sportworks NW
Derick Stevens
Stocks Manufacturing
TerraCycle
Terry Precision Bicycles
Todson
U.S. Public Technologies
University of Illinois
Utah Transit Authority
Claudia Washburn
Dick Weber
Carole Weiss
Chip Williams
Winner International

Special thanks to Randy Neufeld and Tim Herlihey for their support and commitment.

INDEX

A

Access to bike, 24
Accessories, 14–19, 55
Accessory bar, 15
Accident report, 126–129
Accidents, 126–131, 149
Adjuster barrel, 26
Advocacy groups, 64, 130, 200, 233–235
Air pumps, 30
Airless tires, 23
Airplanes, 196–205
Airports, 200
Aluminum wheels, 14, 219
Ambushes, 132
Amtrak, 195
Ankle strap, 14, 189, 231, 233
Armored cables, 59
Armrests, 14, 15
Assertive riding, 123
Attacks, 132, 134–137, 141–145
   by dogs, 144–145
Attorney. *See* Lawyers
Auctions, police, 45
Automobiles. *See* Cars
Axle pegs, 14, 17
Axles, lubrication, 33

B

Back gear assembly, lubrication, 33
Back pain, 8
Backpacks, 229
Baggage
   accessories, 16–17
   bike on airplanes as, 202–205
   bike on trains as, 195
   on buses, 178, 180, 183
Bandanna. *See* Kerchief
Baskets, 14, 17
Batteries, for lights, 211, 212
Bearings, wet, 217
Bells and whistles, 77, 238
Bicycle. *See* Bike
Bike
   on airplanes, 196–205
   as baggage, 195, 205

Bike (continued)
   to carry, 166–167
   in cars, 206
   choosing and fitting, 4–24
   frame height, 13
   holding, in small spaces, 183
   new, 12–13
   parking, 46–51
   price, 6–7, 12
   recycling, 7
   rental, 197, 238
   to ship, 196, 199
   single-speed, 5, 20
   storage, 24
   on trains, 184–195
   types, 4–5
   used, 7, 38
   as vehicle, 133
   weight, 5
Bike-advocacy groups, 64, 130, 200, 233–235
Bike bag, 197
Bike box, 197–199, 202–203, 204–205
   reusing, 205
Bike detectors, 108–113
Bike lanes, 90–91, 115, 173
Bike lock. *See* Locks
Bike-luggage fee, at airport, 197, 204–205
Bike maintenance books, 236
Bike racks
   on buses, 176–182
   for parking, 47
   on trains, 192–193, 195
Bike registries, 40–41, 44, 241
Bike routes, 173
Bike shop, 34
   box from, 198, 199
Body language, 69–71 (*See also* Hand signals)
   vehicles', 72–75
Body position, 4, 8, 9, 10, 13
Books, 236
Box, for air travel. *See* Bike box
Box left turn, 85
Brake cables, 33, 217
Brake levers
   lubrication of, 33
   moving too far, 27
   pressure on, 146

INDEX

Lubrication, 32–33
  of locks, 50
Luggage. *See* Baggage

M

Maintenance, 26–34
  books, 236
  quick check, 26–27
Maps, 173
  to airports, 200
Mechanics at bike shops, 34
Medical attention, 126, 150–151
Medical costs, 131
Merging, 72, 84, 98–99, 119
Messengers, 47
Metal detectors, 109–110
Meters. *See* Parking meters
Michigan left turn, 88–89
Mirror, 14, 68, 116
Money (*See also* Insurance)
  for bike, 6–7, 12, 52
  for bus fare, 183
  for helmet, 227
  for lock, 52
Motorists
  conflicts with, 133, 138–143, 213
  confusing, 141
  crashes with, 126–127
  predicting moves of, 72–73
Mountain bikes, 4–5
Mr. Bike
  contacting, 237
  message from, 1
Multi-lane intersections, 82–84
Multiple speeds. *See* Gears

N

National bike-advocacy groups, 64, 130, 233
Narrow streets. *See* Streets
Neck pain, 8
New bikes, 12–13
New Jersey turn. *See* Jughandle turn
Night riding, 208–213
  danger of, 122–123
Night travel on trains, 194
Noise
  in emergency, 135
  makers, 14, 76–78
Numbness, preventing, 215, 218

O

Oil
  household, 33
  on wet road, 219
Oiling. *See* Lubrication
One-speed bike, 20
One-way streets, 89

P

Packing clothes. *See* Clothing, packing
Padlock, 49, 53, 56, 58
Pain
  in back, arms, or shoulders, 8
  knee, 8, 20
Panniers, 14, 17, 229
Pants, 215, 216, 231
Parked cars, 81, 114–117, 121, 122–123
Parking a bike, 46–51
Parking lots, 46
Parking meters, 47
Parking racks, 46, 193
Partial ped mode, 86
Parts, securing, 49
Passing, 74–75, 80–81
  a bus, 94–97
  on right, 122–123
Patching a tire, 30
Pavement detectors, 108–113
Ped mode, 63, 86, 105–107
Pedals
  clipless, 19
  lubrication, 33
  to rainproof, 217
  speed of, 154, 196
Pedestrian mode. *See* Ped mode
Pedestrian-controlled traffic lights,
  102, 109
Pedestrians
  acting like, 63
  approaching from behind, 78
  between parked cars, 117
  conflicts with, 138–139, 141
  diagonally crossing, 105
  under elevated tracks, 121
Pepper spray, 135–137, 145
  suppliers, 240
Permit for bikes
  on buses, 176
  on trains, 190

INDEX

INDEX

COMMENT FORM

Do you have any comments on this book? If so, please write them on this page. Tear it out and send it to us. Your feedback can help us improve future editions.

_____

_____

_____

_____

_____

_____

_____

If you'd like a reply or want to hear about upcoming books, please tell us how we can contact you. (We won't give this info to anyone else.)

_____
NAME

_____
STREET ADDRESS

_____
CITY, STATE/PROVINCE, ZIP/POSTAL CODE

_____
PHONE

_____
E-MAIL

MAIL TO:

Wordspace Press
2445 North Artesian Avenue
Chicago IL 60647
phone 773/292-0932 voice & fax
comment@wordspacepress.com

Find more info at www.wordspacepress.com

ORDER FORM

_____
NAME

_____
STREET ADDRESS

_____
CITY, STATE/PROVINCE, ZIP/POSTAL CODE

_____
PHONE

_____
E-MAIL

TITLE		QUANTITY	PRICE EACH	TOTAL PRICE
Urban Bikers' Tricks & Tips			$14.95 US	
Kids on Bikes 12-page safety booklet for kids	1 to 49 copies		.85 US	
	50 to 99 copies		.80 US	
	100 or more copies		.75 US	
Bicyclist Survival adult safety booklet	1 to 99 copies		.90 US	
	100 to 499 copies		.85 US	
	500 or more copies		.80 US	

METHOD OF PAYMENT		SUBTOTAL	
		IL RESIDENTS ADD SALES TAX (X 1.065)	
☐ CHECK ☐ MONEY ORDER	SHIP-PING	IA, IL, IN, WI, MO ADD 10% (X 1.1)	
		ALL OTHERS ADD 20% (X 1.2)	
		TOTAL	

MAIL YOUR ORDER TO:

Wordspace Press
2445 North Artesian Avenue
Chicago IL 60647
phone 773/292-0932 voice & fax
orders@wordspacepress.com

Order *Urban Bikers' Tricks & Tips* and our other publications
on-line at www.wordspacepress.com